Let me start by saying that Charlie has some of the most awesome experiences in Jesus; this book is evidence of that. As I read the testimonies and revelations that were shared in the pages of this book, it thrilled my soul. There is innocence to be obtained, and it is reachable if we will just allow God to do His work in us. Jesus, we need a "baptism of innocence"! Thank you, Charlie, for being transparent, as always.

— **Belinda Owens**
Author and Pastor, Glory Barn Branson, Branson, Missouri

My dear friend, Charlie Coker, has given fresh language to Acts 2, and at the same time potentially solved a long-standing schism in the church. Let me explain. Many believers know of and have experimented with the baptism of the Holy Spirit. With that experience has come an awareness of the indwelling presence of the Lord as well as various gifts. On the other side is the group of people who are working to become holy and blameless. Denying the gifts, they live by discipline to keep themselves unspotted from the world. One side emphasizes character; the other is enamored with power—but one is not effective without the other. The baptism of innocence marries the two in a way that reveals the way of the Master. This is a revelation that will open the church up to receive both the purity and the power of Christ. Charlie Coker has a powerful revelation of the grace that makes all things new and reveals the bride adorned in the glory she was born for.

— **Bill Vanderbush**
Author and Pastor of Community Presbyterian Church, Celebration, Florida

The Baptism of Innocence is a high-level revelatory work that will release a wave of reconciliation both within ourselves and with how we perceive others. This book is simultaneously hard-hitting and fun to read. Charlie's personal accounts and style keep the reader engaged while exploring the depths of the finished work of the cross. I recommend *The Baptism of Innocence* for our maturity as believers and as a training tool for sharing the gospel of the kingdom.

— **Dave King**
Author of *Promotion* and Executive Director, Heartsupport Foundation, Senior Associate Leader, Journey Center, Horseheads, New York

In this present day, innocence is rarely spoken of. Perhaps it's because we find it to be elusive and unattainable, and for far too many, innocence has been stolen; for others, it has been given away. No matter the reason or circumstance, the loss of innocence forces us to grow up too quickly, while at the same time stunting our growth. I think innocence is rarely spoken of because we simply just don't want to "go there."

Insert Charlie Coker. Though some may not want to "go there," he is the man for the job. Charlie is a living epistle who is willing to let his pages be read for the good of all. He is not afraid to let us see the ugly parts of his processing, and because of this, we can see that God is there on every page and in every crazy step of our journey. Some of His best lessons are caught in process.

This message of the baptism of innocence is so needed, so relevant, and so healing. Take your time as you read and let Abba submerge the recesses of your soul. As I read through these pages, I had several encounters—at the most unlikely of places! Innocence is assured, if you will give God honest access. May you also reclaim what Jesus died for you to have!

— **Lisa Lowmaster**
Co-Founder, Journey Church, Horseheads, New York

In this book, Charlie Coker presents a truth given to the disciples by our Lord Jesus Christ in Matthew 18:3–4 (NKJV):

Assuredly, I say to you, unless you are converted and become as little children, you will by no means enter the kingdom of heaven. Therefore whoever humbles himself as this little child is the greatest in the kingdom of heaven.

Too often in our "Christian pursuit" of the kingdom of heaven, we have left this place of humility and innocence by complicating the grace found in the gospel. We have taken on the baggage of unforgiveness of ourselves and held others to a standard not held by God. In doing so, we have left the place of innocence found in our first love of Christ.

In sharing the revelation of the baptism of innocence given to Charlie by God, Charlie helps us to re-examine our lives in Christ. By receiving from our Lord this baptism of innocence, we return to that state of childlikeness that brings us into right relationship with Him and the body of Christ. May we all receive this revelation and pursue the baptism of innocence.

— **James Cotton**
Senior Leader, Spirit Alive Church, St. Augustine, Florida

This book is a vital and unique book with a challenging title, by an author who has both experienced, seen, and proved it in personal ministry. The concept is rapidly changing people, restoring long-held broken relationships, and moving many people toward positions that can only be held as components necessary for settling long-existing issues between people.

These words should be seriously examined and quickly applied in the life of every reader, and everyone who reads it will discover the biblical truth of "knowing," which includes an all-out commitment. In turn, heaven suddenly happens on earth! The volume will prove to be a door into such an experience.

— **Jack Taylor**
President, Dimensions Ministries, Melbourne, Florida

To say that *The Baptism of Innocence* is a necessary read for every believer is, in my opinion, the understatement of the millennium. My church gives out Bibles to people who come to the altar when they make a confession of faith. I am going to add this book as another gift to those who receive Jesus. The church has lost the complete message of the cross when it comes to forgiveness—forgiveness of others as well as the forgiveness of self! It has indeed, been PAID IN FULL. *The Baptism of Innocence* is a revelation from God that will advance His kingdom far beyond anything we can imagine. We then come to the full realization that Jesus has not only forgiven us, but he has disposed of the written record that damned us. And when we do that for others, freedom—total freedom in Christ—is the natural outcome. "Love keeps NO RECORD of wrongs." Enjoy, but put your seatbelt on, because you're in for the ride of your life!

— **Matthew Sassano, Jr.**
Lead Pastor, Fresh Start Church, Hornell, New York

Most of us know that innocence and purity start with a new beginning, naturally and spiritually. So many of us love the idea of a brand-new start in our career, new opportunities, maybe a new relationship, or a fresh encounter with God.

Or maybe we are looking for a complete encounter, breakthrough, reboot, or "reset"—a place where all things are made new.

Enter "The Challenge." How do we get there? With so many bad choices, abuses, hurts, pain, rejection, abandonment, bad life experiences, and just plain weariness, we have a difficult time confronting, discovering, or dealing with the people and situations that caused the trauma to begin with.

This is not just a theory, but a reality in facing the difficulty moving forward, especially when it is easier to just walk away, dismiss, or deny that there is any challenge at all. You may even say, "There's nothing to talk about," when in reality, there is not only much to talk about, but much to reconcile and restore.

Lisa and I were eyewitnesses to this taking place at Journey Church when Charlie was at our Accelerant Conference, and we watched the revelation of the Lord break out through this amazing friend of ours. It changed everything for us, our region, and maybe our history. Listen to the journey that my friend takes you on and discover your path forward to the "baptism of innocence." Allow it to be a beautiful weapon of warfare in your challenges: past, present, and future.

— **Scott Lowmaster**
Senior Leader, Journey Church, Horseheads, New York

At a time of emotional weariness and spiritual depletion, we had an unexpected, life-changing prophetic encounter with Charlie, centered around this profound life message he calls "the baptism of innocence." First, Charlie told us his own journey with his battle to extend unconditional and total forgiveness to those who had deeply hurt him and his church. Then he clearly spelled out the meaning and implications of this essential theme in the kingdom. When he was done, we were so convicted that we erased all the records of wrongs we had filed. This act of obedience caused an immediate release of God's manifest presence, favor, and grace. We experienced supernatural freedom and peace once we had extended this "baptism of innocence" to all who had harmed us and those we loved. There aren't enough words to adequately express just how important it is to read and apply the message of this book: *The Baptism of Innocence*.

— **Dr. Timothy and Janet Johns**
Founders of the Rock International "Tribe"

It's not often that an idea or concept is so revelatory that I pick up the phone and make calls. That is precisely what I did when Charlie's message on innocence broke through my world. This is a life-changer—or more correctly, a kingdom-changer. Innocence will restore a measure of the kingdom of God that has been missing. What if we could get this? What would it do if we embraced innocence? The body of Christ would immediately become safer, more pleasing to the Father, and would have an aroma that would attract the world to the church the way fresh bread brings my kids to the kitchen. An overstatement, you say? Not unless innocence was unintended by the Father. But may I remind you of Jesus' words while they were piercing His hands and feet: "Father, forgive them." But He did not stop there, He added, "They know not what they do." He called out for innocence. Charlie Coker has caught a wind shift in the Spirit. So open your sails if you dare. Allow the Wind of God to drive you into the deep—into the uncharted.

— **Brian Higbee**
Author and Senior Leader of CityChurch, Connellsville, Pennsylvania

The *Baptism* of INNOCENCE

A Weapon of Victory
The "Other Side" Series

Charlie Coker

The Baptism of Innocence: A Weapon of Victory

© 2020 by Charlie Coker. All rights reserved.

No part of this book may be reproduced without written permission from the publisher or copyright holder, nor may any part of this book be transmitted in any form or by any means electronic, mechanical, photocopying, recording, or other, without prior written permission from the publisher or copyright holder.

Unless otherwise noted, Scripture quotations are taken from the ESV® Bible (The Holy Bible, English Standard Version®). ESV® Text Edition: 2016. Copyright © 2001 by Crossway, a publishing ministry of Good News Publishers. The ESV® text has been reproduced in cooperation with and by permission of Good News Publishers. Unauthorized reproduction of this publication is prohibited. All rights reserved.

Scripture quotations marked (NKJV) are taken from the New King James Version®. Copyright © 1982 by Thomas Nelson. Used by permission. All rights reserved.

Scripture quotations marked (KJV) are taken from the King James Version, which is in public domain.

Scripture quotations marked (TPT) are taken from The Passion Translation®. Copyright © 2017 by BroadStreet Publishing® Group, LLC. Used by permission. All rights reserved. thePassionTranslation.com.

Printed in the United States of America

ISBN: 978-1-7330786-4-1 (Print)

   978-1-7330786-5-8 (E-book)

Dedication & Acknowledgments

This book is dedicated to my wife, Susan Grace Coker. It has taken a long time for God to explain grace to me, but because so many people around our lives have the middle name "Grace"—you, my mother, our daughter-in-law, our granddaughter, and with your mother's first name being "Grace"—it was about time! Thank you for all the grace you have given to me.

I am so grateful to Bill and Tracie Vanderbush for their influence in my life. You guys brought safety and revelation that has been life-changing. It is a privilege to call you friends.

To Scott and Lisa Lowmaster, senior leaders of the Journey Center in Horseheads, New York. You and your church family have always set an environment of God's presence with a kingdom focus that has set the stage for this book and many more to be written. Thank you for your friendship and for sharing who you are and all you have with Susie and me.

To my church family at Identity Church, I thank you for your support and prayers. I am so proud to be your Pastor. Thanks for putting up with me preaching on innocence until I got it. Love you all.

Last but not least, I want to thank Cathy Sanders with Cathy Sanders Book Design for all her help with the production and editing side of this project. Thank you for helping me keep it professional.

— **Pastor Charlie Coker**

Contents

Foreword by Jim and Mary Baker	13
Introduction	15
Chapter 1: The Revelation of Mary Baker	23
Chapter 2: Learning the Mechanics of Innocence	37
Chapter 3: The Foundation of Innocence Is Love	49
Chapter 4: Forgiven	63
Chapter 5: Shamelessness and Innocence	73
Chapter 6: No Paperwork!	85
Chapter 7: The Boundaries of Grace	99
Chapter 8: Childlikeness Is the Weapon!	111
Chapter 9: It's About the Lamb, Not a Goat	121
Chapter 10: Operational Instructions for the Weapon of Innocence	133

Foreword by Jim and Mary Baker

We met Charlie a few years ago, and it was obvious that he is a spiritual father who also knows how to be a son. He is a man who has scars, but he uses those scars to help and heal others. He is a man who hears God's voice clearly while being anchored in God's Word. We've watched him walk through this baptism of innocence, and we can say that this is not just a teaching; it is an impartation that changes lives—lives like yours and ours.

Have you ever had a drink of water or something thirst-quenching, and you didn't know you were thirsty until it was going down? Charlie's book is that refreshing drink of water for those who are feeling fine. After every chapter, you will say to yourself, "Wow, I needed this!" Here is our experience with this book, and we'll put it in the form of a warning:

- It is full of "pockets of encounter" where you will experience God in a new and fresh way. Forget the stale Christian life you have been living, because these pages will renew and refresh your relationship with God.
- There will be times you are in the middle of a paragraph and weeping may occur.
- There will be times when the goodness of God will pass over you and you will remember the first time you fell in love with Jesus.
- You will release innocence toward people who you didn't even know you were holding captive.
- You will hunger to hear God's voice more.

THE BAPTISM OF INNOCENCE

So read on and enjoy the walls that are about to come crashing down around you.

Get ready for encounters.

Get ready for transformation.

Get ready to see the beauty of Jesus.

Get ready to give away what you've received.

Get ready to live on the right side of the cross.

Get ready for a baptism of innocence.

You were made for more, and this book removes the roadblocks keeping you from entering into the fullness of your destiny.

— Jim & Mary Baker

Senior Leaders, Zion Christian Fellowship, ZionEquip.com

Introduction

In the beginning of 2019, Susie and I were driving up the interstate north of Syracuse in upstate New York for a weekend of personal time and enjoyment. We'd been burning the candle at both ends for a few months proceeding that trip, and we needed some time alone. For years, we'd traveled to upstate New York in the Tug Hill area to go snowmobiling, but with warmer temperatures creeping into winter the last few years, you couldn't plan a trip and be sure that there would be snow. So after a good northern snowfall, I purchased expensive plane tickets at a moment's notice, booked lodging, rented snowmobiles, and made it happen (a good way to earn some "brownie points").

We were driving down the highway with ice forming on the car and snow falling all around us—adventurous for a couple of Floridians enjoying the scenery. Susie, my bride of forty years, looked over her left shoulder at me, and it seemed as though her eyes were piercing my soul as she said: "Thank you for making this weekend happen. It sure is better being on the other side of bankruptcy, isn't it?"

Nine years ago we went bankrupt. There's a point in time for every person when their faith is tested. Mine was the bankruptcy. Our business failed. That was a catastrophic moment in my life. It crushed my emotions, hurt my bank account, and shook my faith. It took me years to get over it.

As soon as Susie said, "on the other side," I had a Holy Spirit encounter where the Lord downloaded a folder with twenty-one files inside of it. The title on the folder was "On the Other Side Series."

THE BAPTISM OF INNOCENCE

It's like I instantly knew that these were all messages for me to preach during the next season of my ministry. Twenty-one messages about pain and failures and mistakes—all tied in to the proper perspective that the other side of the cross changes everything.

I used to criticize people who went bankrupt until I had to face it myself, and then I had to repent for doing so. We had fought bankruptcy for years, and some years were very hard. The crisis changed our lives and gave us new tools to help others learn that God is faithful. I found that the other side of bankruptcy is better.

"On the other side" has become a theme wherever I go now. I've discovered that there is something that everyone needs to get on the other side of. What is it that you can't get past? I've been pastoring for years and counseling people on some of these issues, so I know that many deal with a lot of issues that they have a hard time getting on the other side.

I want you to take a minute and do an inventory of your lives. Write out "On the other side of _____" and fill in the blank. For some, it might be divorce. For others, it might be a moral failure. It might be the death of a spouse, or the death of a family member. A few other thoughts: shame and public humiliation, an educational crisis, a medical situation (cancer, kidney failure, liver, lungs, thyroid, emotional issues, etc.). Some may be on the other side of a church failure, or a spiritual leadership failure. There are so many things that could go in the blank that people cannot seem to get past. You may have a list of five or six things, or even more, that you can't get past—write them all down.

Whatever has hindered your ability to see Jesus in the dimension of who He really is, whatever has stolen your hope, write it down. When your hope is gone, you can't see Jesus through the proper filter. Some of you need to write "on the other side of the fight with my spouse today." Make your list.

You have to get to the point where you draw a line in the sand and get on the other side of it. Once you're on the other side of that thing,

INTRODUCTION

you can rule it—it's not ruling you any longer. You can rule on the other side of something, but you've got to know that you're *on* the other side.

Here's the crux of it: Are you on the other side of the cross? If you don't recognize that you're on the other side of the cross, the thing that tried to steal your hope is still robbing you of joy and peace, and you're still under its oppression. That is why I wrote this book—to help you get to the other side of the cross in those issues that you wrote down.

Jesus's Visitations

Let's look at the first three visitations of Jesus to His disciples after the finished work of the cross. You can find all of these encounters in John chapters 19–21.

The apostle John was part of Jesus's inner circle when he wrote his book fifty years after the resurrection. So what we have is a bunch of older saints sitting around reminiscing about what made them successful in the kingdom. These disciples turned the world upside-down after Jesus died, correct? They transformed the world, and then decades later, they gave us tools to get on the other side of things that hider us and show us how to function in miraculous power. Jesus said, "It is finished," and then He got on the other side of the cross and gave us the mandate to do what He did.

The first three files in the folder that God downloaded to me were about the first three visitations Jesus had with His disciples on the other side of the cross. These encounters tell a very different story about what Jesus accomplished and the tools He's given us.

The First Encounter

The first encounter happened when the apostles were commissioned.

> On the evening of that day, the first day of the week, the doors being locked where the disciples were for fear of the Jews, Jesus came and stood among them and said to them,

THE BAPTISM OF INNOCENCE

> "Peace be with you." When he had said this, he showed them his hands and his side. Then the disciples were glad when they saw the Lord. Jesus said to them again, "Peace be with you. As the Father has sent me, even so I am sending you." And when he had said this, he breathed on them and said to them, "Receive the Holy Spirit. If you forgive the sins of any, they are forgiven them; if you withhold forgiveness from any, it is withheld" (John 20:19–23).

This was the first encounter that the disciples had with Jesus on the other side of the cross. Not only was it a commissioning, but also a new mandate for how to function in this new kingdom protocol and do greater works than Jesus had done in His earthly ministry. He simply said, "As the Father has sent me, even so I am sending you." Then He gave them power to forgive sin. That's greater than Jesus did, because we were crucified with Christ, and He gave us the power to forgive sin—a one-time crucifixion for all mankind. Another key in this encounter is that He gave them peace that cancels fear.

The Second Encounter

Jesus shows himself in the corporate setting with a personal agenda to help Thomas believe.

> Now Thomas, one of the twelve, called the Twin, was not with them when Jesus came. So the other disciples told him, "We have seen the Lord." But he said to them, "Unless I see in his hands the mark of the nails and place my finger into the mark of the nails, and place my hand into his side, I will never believe" (John 20:24–25).

Look at the two demands that Thomas makes before he will believe: to see the marks in His hands and touch the wound in His side. After such a brutal crucifixion, Jesus would have had thousands of scars on His body—ripped flesh from the beating of the cat of nine tails to the scars from the crown of thorns being pressed into His head. But after the finished work of the cross, Jesus only showed the two scars that Thomas

INTRODUCTION

demanded to see and touch. When the finished work of the cross has done its job, scars are optional, and should only be used to assist others in believing the finished work of the cross and the risen Christ. My identity is not in my scars, but in Christ.

> Eight days later, his disciples were inside again, and Thomas was with them. Although the doors were locked, Jesus came and stood among them and said, "Peace be with you." Then he said to Thomas, "Put your finger here, and see my hands; and put out your hand, and place it in my side. Do not disbelieve, but believe." Thomas answered him, "My Lord and my God!" Jesus said to him, "Have you believed because you have seen me? Blessed are those who have not seen and yet have believed."
>
> Now Jesus did many other signs in the presence of the disciples, which are not written in this book; but these are written so that you may believe that Jesus is the Christ, the Son of God, and that by believing you may have life in his name (John 20:26–31).

The Third Encounter

> After this Jesus revealed himself again to the disciples by the Sea of Tiberias, and he revealed himself in this way. Simon Peter, Thomas (called the Twin), Nathanael of Cana in Galilee, the sons of Zebedee, and two others of his disciples were together. Simon Peter said to them, "I am going fishing." They said to him, "We will go with you." They went out and got into the boat, but that night they caught nothing (John 21:1–3).

Many times, we have a crisis with how Jesus is running His kingdom, so we go back to what we're familiar with and operate in our own strength. But when we recognize that what we are doing isn't fruitful, we need to look for Jesus.

THE BAPTISM OF INNOCENCE

> Just as day was breaking, Jesus stood on the shore; yet the disciples did not know that it was Jesus. Jesus said to them, "Children, do you have any fish?" They answered him, "No." He said to them, "Cast the net on the right side of the boat, and you will find some." So they cast it, and now they were not able to haul it in, because of the quantity of fish. That disciple whom Jesus loved therefore said to Peter, "It is the Lord!" When Simon Peter heard that it was the Lord, he put on his outer garment, for he was stripped for work, and threw himself into the sea. The other disciples came in the boat, dragging the net full of fish, for they were not far from the land, but about a hundred yards off (John 21:4–8).

Jesus had finished His assignment to deal with sin on the earth. Jesus would not let Mary touch Him at the gravesite until He had returned to the Father in heaven, where sin originated with the rebellion with Lucifer. Jesus dealt with sin at its beginning. So when Jesus showed up on the beach, we see a shift in how He addressed His followers. He didn't call them disciples. He was fully God, and He called them "children." Then He gave them an instruction that was different from their professional opinion on how to catch fish. But the great harvest of fish revealed that it was the Lord on the bank.

> When they got out on land, they saw a charcoal fire in place, with fish laid out on it, and bread. Jesus said to them, "Bring some of the fish that you have just caught." So Simon Peter went aboard and hauled the net ashore, full of large fish, 153 of them. And although there were so many, the net was not torn. Jesus said to them, "Come and have breakfast." Now none of the disciples dared ask him, "Who are you?" They knew it was the Lord. Jesus came and took the bread and gave it to them, and so with the fish. This was now the third time that Jesus was revealed to the disciples after he was raised from the dead (John 21:9–14).

INTRODUCTION

This third encounter was a corporate display of the Godhead and responsibility Jesus gave us. These professional fishermen fished all night and caught nothing. As the unrevealed Jesus was on the bank giving instruction to fish "on the other side," it was the first time He called them "children," and then He asked for a portion of their fish to use to make breakfast for them all. When Jesus walked on the earth, He took five loaves and two fish to feed over five thousand people.

On the other side of the cross, Jesus gives us authority to forgive sin, the ability to show the scars of life for someone else's benefit, and then He tells us to operate the same way that He did in miracles, signs, and wonders. He puts miracles in our hands as we obey His voice.

Chapter 1: The Revelation of Mary Baker

A Year-Long Frustration

I was invited to speak at the Accelerant Conference in March of 2018 in Horseheads, New York. I was asked to put out a Facebook video post ahead of time to promote the conference. I had the lineup of who was speaking—Jack Taylor, Bill Vanderbush, Charlie Coker—you know, the "greats." Then there was picture of a guy by the name of "Jim Baker." I had never met him before, so in the video (being the smart aleck that I am) I said, "I hope he's not married to Tammy Faye," and I posted it on Facebook. I knew he wasn't, but when I posted that video, I suddenly went into a vision and God gave me prophetic insight about the region Jim and Mary Baker lived in and the authority that God was giving them.

I didn't know what Jim's wife's name was in the natural, however, I knew her name prophetically. God gave me a detailed download for them and the region they lived in. It is interesting that I had a very similar word about that same region several years earlier. As I finished writing it out, the Lord said to me, "When you go to the conference and it's your turn to preach, I want you to prophesy this to them publicly." It was a personal word and also a corporate release for regional authority, plus a personal word of private information for Mary Baker.

So I went to the conference, knowing that I was to be an agent of change; I was to release a corporate shift from the heavenly realm to bring change. I was excited! The one big problem was that when it was my turn to preach, the Bakers weren't there yet!

I thought, *Did I miss the whole thing?* But the Lord confirmed to me that I hadn't missed it. There was a row of seats where all the speakers sit, and each chair had names on the chairs for who was supposed to sit there. Because the Bakers hadn't arrived yet, their chairs were empty. The Lord said, "Set the two chairs in front of the pulpit with their names on them, and prophesy over their chairs." So when it was my turn to speak, I prophesied over two empty chairs with Jim and Mary Baker's names on them. Bill Vanderbush was sending videos to Jim, saying, "Hey, this prophet is prophesying over you and Mary." At first Jim thought it was a joke, and he said, "Tell him to call Mary's sin out." But when he saw the video, he realized it was for real.

The Bakers came in later that night and were given a copy of the message. The next morning I was able to meet them, and I gave Mary the personal word God had given me for her. There was an instant, God-ordained connection between her and I, and all I could think was that *she scared me.* There was a holy anointing mixed with the weighty glory of God on her life that scared me. She made me feel unworthy, not because of anything about her specifically, but being around her caused me to feel so unworthy on the inside. She emanated a heavenly anointing that I now know as "innocence," but back then I didn't know what to call it. This godly character about her put holy fear in me. I made a conscious decision that there was no way that I could be in any long-term relationship with these two people because I'm too rough around the edges; I didn't have the innocence they carried. So I consciously walled my heart off to them out of my own fears of rejection.

After the meeting, I went out to dinner with Jim, Mary, and Bill Vanderbush. In the middle of a conversation, Mary made an innocent statement and said, "Yeah, I tried wine once when I was on a mission trip in Turkey.

I asked, "What did you think?"

She replied, "Well, my first thought was, 'Why would you put turpentine in a good glass of grape juice?'"

I laughed at that, but inside I was thinking, *Oh my God! This couple has served God from their youth. They came out of the womb singing "holy, holy, holy."* (pardon my "Coker humor"!) With my own history, I said to myself, "I can't be in relationship with Mary and Jim Baker. They're too holy for me. I've been around a lot of ministers who have a religious spirit on them, and I will pick a fight with that spirit if I need to!"

I soon found that this was not the case with Jim and Mary. I wanted to label them as religious, but they were different—they weren't judgmental or boastful; they were completely loving and graceful. They both have a good sense of humor and were a blast to be around. But God used this to expose something wrong inside of me—not them. God was putting His finger on something inside of me, and I knew that the Lord was going to make me wrestle with Him to find out what it was. Mary Baker petrified me in the core of my spirit with fear I had not experienced in many years, and I couldn't put my finger on what it was.

Then the Lord asked me if I trusted Him. I told Him that I did, and then He assured me that I could trust Jim and Mary with my heart, fears, and calling. That didn't bring comfort to me—it only ramped up the fear! God was after something in the core of my belief system, and I was not comfortable at all.

The next morning Mary said she had a dream about me, and I was thinking, *Oh God, keep her away from me!* I could see that the Lord was prophetically starting to knit our hearts to one another in the way only God can do. The word was very encouraging, and God was dealing with some of my past so that I could advance into my future.

As I left for home from the weekend of ministry, the Lord told me that I would have to wrestle for the truth and be willing to be vulnerable to Him and others. He said that the core issues I was dealing with will change my life and ministry, and position me to fulfill my destiny.

THE BAPTISM OF INNOCENCE

Unlikely Weapons

Two weeks later, I had a prophetic dream from the Lord. In this dream, Jim and Mary Baker were beating me with weapons. They were abusing me using the weapons—they were tearing me up! As they were banging on me and beating me, I started screaming, "Jesus, save me! They're abusing me!" I was screaming, "Jesus, save me from Jim and Mary Baker!" Jesus walked into the room with a stern look and said, "Stand up! Charles Layton Coker Jr, stand on your feet!"

Now when the Lord called me by my full name, I knew I was in trouble!

As I stood up, He said, "What's your problem?"

I replied, "Jim and Mary are beating me with these weapons!"

He said, "Weapons? Look at their weapons, Charlie."

As I turned to take a closer look at the weapons they were using, I was shocked to see that Mary was beating me with purity and Jim was beating me with holiness. As the revelation unfolded, it was astounding to me that I was being tormented by God's character and nature, and that I had called them weapons of abuse. As the encounter ended, I started repenting and asked forgiveness for judging Jim and Mary, but the Lord stopped me. He said, "You weren't judging them, you were judging ME! It's not a sin issue with you; it's a belief issue. You have believed a lie from the enemy, and you don't believe that I am as good as I truly am. You don't have the total revelation or proper knowledge of the gospel and what I accomplished and completed on the cross. You have lived on the wrong side of the cross most of your walk. Today, that changes."

Operation Avoidance

I've wrestled with that encounter for almost a year. My oldest son, Jason, is pursuing his PhD in Adult Learning. One of the theories he focuses on is perspective transformation and how the underlying beliefs a person has determine their behaviors. Many times, our behaviors do not line up with our stated beliefs. When we realize this, we experience a "disorienting dilemma" that causes psychological stress. When this happens, a person has three options:

1. Decide the stated beliefs and assumptions made are valid and decide to change one's behaviors to align with those beliefs.
2. Decide the stated beliefs and assumptions made are not valid and decide to change one's beliefs and assumptions to align with current behaviors.
3. Ignore the gap between belief and behaviors, and avoid any activity or person who brings awareness to the divide between them.

Most of us choose that third option of avoidance. I had the bright idea that God brought this crisis with the Bakers into my life to help me lean into Him and learn that my behavior was not lining up with what I said I believed, thought was Bible-based, and preached loud and clear. I have discovered that I had a lot of hidden assumptions that the Lord was dealing with.

Back to the Honeymoon

I was invited back to the Accelerant Conference in March 2019, and as I was preparing the messages, the Lord impressed on me to preach the first three messages of the "other-side encounters" that I shared in the Introduction of this book. I felt confident about what I would be preaching. But while I was in prayer a few days before I left for New York, the Lord said to me, "I want to show you something to add to your message." He showed me the folder with the twenty-one files in it and told me to look at the message in file number twelve. So I opened up file number twelve, and the subject line was listed as "The Revelation of Mary Baker." It had the title of this book: "The Baptism of Innocence: A Weapon of Victory," along with several chapters and an outline for this book.

As I prayed over the information, the Holy Spirit hovered over me and baptized me with the "baptism of innocence." I was completely free from shame and guilt, and the fear that I'd been wrestling with for years was gone! I felt the love and embrace of the Father, and a cleansing of my spirit that I had felt twenty-three years earlier during an encounter in which Jesus walked through a wall and gave me a new heart. It was back—the honeymoon was back!

That's when I realized that this "innocence" thing had been stolen from me! I took the information and began to recall the "honeymoon stages" I had been on with God twenty-three years ago. I recognized that I'd been on a religious "hamster wheel," and the Lord brought back to my mind different encounters that I'd had with Him. I recalled what He showed me about shame, how Jesus was naked on the cross and yet He was not ashamed. He took my public humiliation away; He took the shame of my past; He took my sins.

Listen, here's the issue: when Jesus takes your sin and forgives you of your sin, there's this demonic thing on the inside that tries to say, "There just wasn't enough evidence to convict me." But if Jesus only took my sin away, then I'm still stuck with my reputation—I'm stuck with my history (And believe me, have I got history!).

In 1993, Jesus walked through the wall and said, "You're forgiven; you're innocent!" That's what He tells all of us who have accepted Him as Savior. What happens is that we stop at "forgiven" and we don't get to "innocence." We don't go to the completed work of the cross and walk in the innocence He gave us. You may not feel as though you are innocent, and maybe the devil has lied to you about it, but you are innocent.

I had the baptism of innocence for the first couple of years after I got saved, but then I allowed religion to steal it from me for twenty-five years before getting it back. I was so pure and holy the first couple of years that Susie didn't even like me! I had come to the understanding that I was walking in innocence, and Susie rejected me, just like I rejected Mary Baker. But somehow, religion snuck back in. Religion put me on the hamster wheel of trying to please God when God was already pleased with me and had declared me innocent. I started believing religious lies, and it warped my belief system and tainted my ability to see how good God really is.

The Power to Forgive

So I had this life-changing revelation, and now it was time to preach. Fifteen minutes prior to preaching, I was praying, "Lord, are you going to anoint this message?"

He said, "Probably not."

I said, "Lord, that's not funny!

But He was very serious. He said, "Charles Layton Coker Jr., if you fail this test, you will never preach again!" He had my attention again with my whole name. Then the Lord asked, "Did you receive the baptism of innocence on Tuesday?"

I answered, "Yeah."

He said, "Prove it."

"How do I do that?" I asked.

He replied, "If you can't give it away, then you don't have it."

The Lord continued, "Many have been forgiven. Then why do you always argue and debate and carry on about unforgiveness? If you've been forgiven, why do you still carry unforgiveness toward others? Here's the problem, Charlie. When someone does you wrong, you have a hard time forgiving them. The biggest thing is that you don't want to be hurt again. So I hold that same unforgiveness against you."

The Lord started showing me that the first corporate encounter on the other side of the cross to His disciples happened in John 20, when He breathed on them to receive the Holy Spirit and told them, "If you forgive the sins of any, they are forgiven them; if you retain the sins of any, they are retained" (John 20:23 NKJV).

In other words, if you have the Holy Spirit inside of you, you have the power to forgive sin. But we continue to carry unforgiveness toward people and wonder why we are defeated and tormented by the enemy.

As I looked across the room, I saw Randy, my old friend and ex-spiritual son sitting in the third row.

THE BAPTISM OF INNOCENCE

Four years ago, Randy made some very bad choices and ruined many relationships in New York, wound up in an adulterous situation, and got divorced. It happened with one of the girls in the church we were preaching at, and it was a mess. My leadership and I had to make some very hard and painful decisions. A lot of mistakes had been made on all sides, and we tried to work through it, but I felt that I could not walk with Randy any longer, and he felt the same way.

So right after God asked me to prove if I had received the baptism of innocence and instructed me to forgive, there was my longtime friend and ex-spiritual son, who had blamed and hurt me just as much as I had hurt him. The Lord said, "If Randy and you have forgiven each other enough to be in the same room, can you go declare him innocent?"

I asked, "Can I do it after I preach?"

He said, "No. If you don't do it now, you're done."

"But, Lord," I argued, "do you know what he did? Do you know I had to put my reputation on the line to salvage the people group that he had destroyed?"

As I argued with the Lord, I saw in the Spirit all this paperwork with a list of everything Randy had done to me and others. I was in a crisis, and the internal pain of the past was manifesting on the inside of me. I used it to make my case with the Lord and said, "God, look at what he did—look at the paperwork."

God replied, "Did I declare you innocent?"

"Yes."

"Then, go give it away."

The problem was that I had to preach in ten minutes—and now I was cornered by God. He said, "Don't get hung up in the mechanics. Just obey Me."

After having the baptism of innocence three days earlier, there was this childlikeness that gave me the ability to trust the Father. When it came time for me to preach, I walked up to Randy and I said, "Randy, we've forgiven each other to the point that we can be in the same room. But I declare you innocent."

Randy broke. We both started crying and told each other that we loved each other. It was a very impacting and emotional moment.

Then I asked God, "What about all the other people who got hurt? What about my reputation?"

He simply replied, "Oh yeah, I took care of that on the cross. Declare him innocent, then preach about it."

So that night I preached this message about the other side of the cross, and I taught about the baptism of innocence, and publicly declared him innocent.

Randy's Story

After much prayer and consideration, I've come to the conclusion that there is not much for me to say other than it is true that I committed adultery and destroyed my ministry. I hurt a lot of people, and I was also deeply wounded by the church. In the process, I gravely damaged my relationship with my best friend and spiritual father, Charlie Coker, to the point that our fifteen-year relationship seemed irredeemable—not only to me, but to all who were involved.

As Charlie said previously, both of us loved God and were trying to be obedient to His Word. We had forgiven each other enough to be in the same room, but I was sure there would never be any restoration of what we had lost, to the point where I had declared it out of my mouth on more than one occasion. After all, it had been four years since I fell, and we could barely be in the same room together, even though there were times when I missed him more than I could admit.

Years later on March 4, the woman I fell with (who is now my wife) said to me, "God says, 'You need to go to the Accelerant Conference, and I have paid for your ticket.'" To say I didn't want to go is an understatement. Charlie was speaking, and this was also my wife's home church when we fell. When we worked up the courage to admit our sin privately to the leaders there and ask them to walk the process out with us, I was declared by many in the region a wolf in the body of Christ that needed to be murdered. I was not expecting a warm reception.

I really did not want to go back there, but I trusted my wife and went. Papa had a miracle in store for me that I could not see coming. He declares that He will set a table for us in the presence of our enemies. God was using the same man who had rejected and abandoned me—who had helped to destroy all that I had built, in the same place where I first fell in the eyes of the church—to bring restoration and healing. Charlie was the only one who could do it. The only man God could use to murder the flesh out of me, so I would finally be free of that idol that I had spent over twenty years crying out to the Lord to deliver me from. I had used religion to hide that it was still there and to keep me pure, but God wanted it uprooted and taken out. Only Charlie could murder my flesh, because he was the only man I had given my heart to in total trust. It is so amazing to me that God would use the same man who had betrayed my heart of trust, to restore me before the region. Isn't that God?

I don't blame Charlie; I now know it was a God-setup. In the darkness of my cave, I was sitting in my chair, devastated and contemplating suicide, a friend brought to me a book called *Exquisite Agony* by Gene Edwards. It's about the honor of being crucified with Christ and details how Christ was crucified at the hands of His family. Each person was hand-picked by God to bring about not only my freedom, but also to affect an entire region. Charlie was just playing his part; how could I blame him? He was using the Word of God. Even Paul said not to eat with such a one as me. Charlie wasn't at fault; he was just catching up to this message of innocence. This revelation was about to challenge a lot of religious spirits. As Jesus hung on the cross, His final act was to pray, "Father, forgive them, for they know not what they do." It was an act of declaring innocence.

When Charlie came to me that morning in March with tears in his eyes, he said to me, "You may not understand what I am about to share, but I declare you innocent." For a split second I wondered what he was up to. I didn't trust him. He looked me straight in the eye and declared me innocent of all wrongdoing. Then something broke in me, and I think in him as well. Something supernatural was taking place.

Charlie then went on to minister, as this took place in the moments before his time slot at the conference. He told our story with as little detail needed to accomplish Papa's goal, again declaring me innocent before everyone seated there, including leaders and ministers who knew our story and had paperwork against me. After Charlie's declaration over me, the theme of the conference took on John 20:23: "If you forgive the sins of any, they are forgiven them; if you retain the sins of any, they are retained," which are the words of Jesus. Every speaker at the conference made a point to minister to me after that. God began pouring out to me love, healing, and restoration over the next days of the conference. Leif Hetland sealed all that had been done, and spoke over me with a kiss on the final night, imparting the love of God so tangibly that it continued to minister to me.

That declaration from Charlie's tear-filled eyes had started something that I despaired might never come: the restoration of ministry and relationships, along with the cleansing of reproach and shame in the region. Now, twelve months later, my relationship with Charlie is fully restored, as well as with many other regional ministers. We just had our first conference with Charlie, and it was powerful! During the conference I was able to look at Charlie and tell him from a humbled heart, "I trust you." That's something I thought would never be restored again. For months after Charlie's public declaration of innocence over me, we talked more and more often about this mystery of the kingdom. I believe this has been one of the missing keys to completing sonship.

This revelation is taking on a life of its own and spreading throughout the body. As a pastor and prophet, there's a whole lot more that I could say after a year of living this innocence message out, but this is Charlie's book so I will end with: WOW! Look what the Lord has done! Of course, there are still those who are looking from the sidelines and watching, waiting to see how this innocence thing plays out; those who aren't ready to declare me innocent. I declare them innocent and release them to receive this revelation for themselves. All I now know is that I have fallen captive into the loving arms of my Father once again.

—*Randy & Amanda Hughes*

Don't Feed the Wrong Dog!

There are people in leadership there who don't think that Randy is innocent—forgiven, maybe, but not innocent. I'm still in their conference and under their authority. The power of the cross that makes you innocent is going to confront your religious dance.

When you are a leader, there is a greater responsibility to walk in a worthy manner before the Lord and the body of Christ. At the same time, many have had failures and never returned to ministry. I don't believe that it's the will of the Father for that to be the norm. I believe this message will heal, clean, and empower many leaders who are still hiding in the cave of rejection and despair. It's time to become our brother's keeper and help others get back in the family business of bringing heaven to earth. We need them. They have learned some things in the cave that we need in the body of Christ. The baptism of innocence will facilitate this recovery and keep us on the path with Jesus, while allowing us to walk it out with purity and power.

Many people have taken the Scriptures to war in prayer and declared "I'm righteous" because of the righteousness that Jesus gave, and started declaring, "My words are righteous words; I've never seen the righteous forsaken or His seed begging for bread." But if our righteousness involves even a tiny bit of our own works, then it is not founded on innocence. If you have to work for any part of it, it becomes self-righteousness and not His righteousness. When He says, "You're righteous," it's completely about Him. The foundation of real righteousness is that you're innocent, which becomes the weapon of war.

I was raised in an Assemblies of God church with the belief that we had two dogs in our lives: a good dog and a bad dog. If we're not walking with Jesus, we're feeding the wrong dog. Let me tell you something: if you're innocent, the dog is dead! There is no bad dog on the inside—it's dead! The problem is that we haven't received the baptism of innocence from the Father, therefore we walk around in condemnation and guilt. Remember, you're innocent!

The weapon of childlikeness and removing paperwork are true mysteries of the kingdom, both supernatural to the core and life-changing.

I had to personally receive the baptism of innocence and walk it out first. God confronted me and my beliefs to bring change in our behavior. God chose to confront my behavior with Randy to heal that relationship. This unlocked a new set of mysteries of the kingdom. This is not a corporate formula that every relationship has to walk through. Only God can show you the steps for your own baptism of innocence. There are some relationships that may never be reinstated, but the baptism of innocence will bring healing and closure to your heart, and will open up the kingdom in new dimensions to you.

***

Wisdom Keys:

1. The baptism of innocence is for you personally first; let it do its work in you before you give it away.
2. Be careful not to judge people as religious when it's really innocence.
3. The dog is dead—Stop resurrecting it.
4. Faith is born out of innocence.

Chapter 2: Learning the Mechanics of Innocence

As I began learning more about the baptism of innocence, I was reminded of Proverbs 25:2, which says, "It is the glory of God to conceal things, but the glory of kings is to search things out." In this chapter, I will share the experiences I had with God, and how living out the baptism of innocence changed some mechanics of my day-to-day life.

Jesus started off saying, "Do you want Me to be really blunt with you?" When I said yes, the Lord asked, "Do you promise not to get mad with me? When you got saved, and had your encounter with me when I walked through the wall, were you addicted to pornography and many other things?

I replied to Him, "Lord, You know I was in a demonic lifestyle, and my Achilles heel was porn, which destroyed everything around me."

He said, "Give me your report card on porn for the last twenty-five years."

I gave that to Him. I had three mistakes; not seasons, mistakes. I have watched porn only three times in twenty-five years.

He responded, "That's pretty good. In man's standards, that would be an A." Then He said to me, "But if you had understood and continued to walk in the revelation of innocence like you did the first few years, you wouldn't have needed a report card, because there would have been no test."

THE BAPTISM OF INNOCENCE

"What?" I answered God. "Do You know how hard I've worked to walk in holiness and purity? How hard I've prayed and used the sword of the Spirit, prayed and fasted and did warfare? I've got friends I'd call and say, 'Hey, I'm struggling, I'm being tempted.' I had accountability!" I had no idea there was a way to not have a test.

The Lord said, "Porn loses its attraction when you are baptized in innocence. It no longer has an attraction because you're innocent. The ability to resist is empowered by innocence, and innocence will turn a weakness into a strength. But an unguarded strength will become a double weakness, so always keep the door to the enemy closed up tight with the lock of innocence."

This works with any struggle. Just replace the word *porn* with whatever it is you struggle with: anger, covetousness, pride, etc. You can't be prideful and innocent at the same time. You can't be innocently prideful either!

> And they were bringing children to him that he might touch them, and the disciples rebuked them. But when Jesus saw it, he was indignant and said to them, "Let the children come to me: do not hinder them, for to such belongs the kingdom of God. Truly, I say to you, whoever does not receive the kingdom of God like a child shall not enter it." And he took them in his arms and blessed them, laying his hands on them (Mark 10:13–16).

The problem is that we've applied the cross to remove our sin, and said, "Yay! My sins are gone!" But we never took that next step and became innocent like a child. Therefore we can't enter into the mystery of the kingdom where innocence lives. He wouldn't tell us to come to Him as a child if He didn't give us the ability to be childlike. The perversion that would have destroyed us, and that we have to wrestle against, goes away when we become innocent.

LEARNING THE MECHANICS OF INNOCENCE

The Many-Breasted One

One of the words the Lord gave me at the beginning of the 2020 was that He was releasing the anointing of the "Many-Breasted One."

The Friday night before Christmas, I was out with my wife, and I told her that I would really like to get a massage on Saturday. So she booked a session for me, a ninety-minute massage at 10:00 a.m. This would be the first of ten vacation days I would have from Christmas to the New Year. So on Saturday I got up, had my coffee, and was having a good time with the Lord. I had to run a few errands before getting my massage.

As I was driving, I was listening to a country music station, and they were playing Christmas songs. I was worshipping with "O Holy Night" and it felt like God had showed up in my car. Then a well-known country song came on that caught me off guard. It broke the spirit of worship and was the biggest buzzkill ever. It truly made me mad! How could some radio jockey change from "O Holy Night" to that song and think that was cool? The whole song talked about how breaking up with a boyfriend is like a girl taking her bra off and how it feels so freeing. As the song continued to play, it broke my worship and totally made me angry!

I was supposed to be getting ready for ninety minutes of relaxation and stress removal. I started to get quiet, and the Lord asked me why that song made me so mad. He reminded me of the fact that it was on a secular station and that type of message is part of our culture, and told me that it shouldn't make me angry. He also impressed that if the church wants to change the culture around them, then we need to embrace it and change it from the inside—not by being angry and throwing rocks at it from the outside.

Then He told me, "Open your heart; you asked for a word for the year for you and the church—here it is!

"This is the year when the "El Shaddai" ("Many-Breasted One") anointing will be released to the church and the nurturing side of God will become the foundation of a great harvest. He said, "I am taking the bra off My bride and setting her free from the religious restraints so I can nurture, heal, and return proper identity to the body of Christ. Young and old need to embrace Me in My nurturing anointing to help return to childlikeness."

The Lord reminded me that Jesus was born in a different culture, and for Him to fulfill His purpose it had to start off in His infancy. Then He asked me what I thought Mary did when He was feeding from her breast? Mary would look into His eyes as Jesus was getting nourishment in the natural, and she would speak to Him about His identity, purpose, and value. She would retell the stories of how the angels named Him and how she was told what would become of Him and why. The Lord reminded me that Jesus was born in a different culture, and for Jesus to fulfill His purpose, it had to start off in His infancy.

The Lord told me that if Mary had only used the feeding time to only stop the cry of an infant and not use it to impart destiny and purpose, Jesus would have been immature, lacking proper identity, and His developmental process would have been hindered to the point where He may not have been able to complete His calling.

The Lord told me that the body of Christ was entering a season of detox from the effects of drinking from the religious spirit. That is why so many people have lost their passion and purpose. There have been some in the body of Christ who have lost their way, and after the detox has been completed, clarity will come back as the "El Shaddai," the mothering side of God, will become the place of intimacy and nourishment. Childlikeness will return to the body and become one of the major foundational truths for the harvest that will change the culture around us.

The Lord is breaking up with religion, and when He has taken the bra off the bride of Christ, the nurturing side of God will become a public manifestation of pure childlikeness, from the young to the old. The day will come when the world will say that the church has found its purpose, with power and purity.

LEARNING THE MECHANICS OF INNOCENCE

Returning to Childlikeness

Some of us are so proud of our accomplishments as adults, but it's not founded on the innocence that Christ gave us at the finished work of the cross. Therefore, we're still on that hamster wheel of religion. While God was teaching me this, I asked Him, "But, God, how do I handle wrong behavior and deal with the "Randy" situations?" This behavior was destructive in nature. He said, "Son, first of all, there was repentance, which opens the door for relationship and accountability with safety protocols set up so as to not repeat the behavior. But your love starts with a declaration of innocence, which gives you and Randy a clean slate to work from. Don't avoid weakness, or it will be repeated. Innocence will openly reveal the unhealed areas, and submitting one to another will not happen until that area has been brought into maturity. If both are walking in innocence, it will be a two-way street and not just one sided.

Then the Lord gave me an example. He said, "You don't hand your car keys to a twelve-year-old even though they will eventually learn how to drive. You wait and bring them to maturity. But if they only behave because they want to drive rather than learning the principles of driving, then you're handing them a time bomb."

When someone doesn't understand that they are innocent in God's eyes, then their identity is skewed. But when childlikeness enters the relationship, changes will come, and that person will submit to others to cover areas that need maturing. That's when they become their brother's keeper.

The bottom line is: either Jesus became our sin and declared us innocent, or He didn't. I've preached messages that let people know that I sin just like everyone else, but when the video evidence is viewed in heaven, Jesus says, "Oh, that video of Charlie? I'll cover him in My blood." Then the screen turns red and Jesus becomes my loophole. The real fact is that He *became* my sin.

> All this is from God, who through Christ reconciled us to himself and gave us the ministry of reconciliation; that

is, in Christ God was reconciling the world to himself, not counting their trespasses against them, and entrusting to us the message of reconciliation. Therefore, we are ambassadors for Christ, God making his appeal through us. We implore you on behalf of Christ, be reconciled to God. For our sake he made him to be sin who knew no sin, so that in him we might become the righteousness of God (2 Corinthians 5:18–21).

Look at what *The Passion Translation* says about this concept:

And He chose us to be his very own, joining us to himself even before he laid the foundation of the universe! Because of his great love, he ordained us, so that we would be seen as holy in his eyes with an unstained innocence (Eph. 1:4 TPT).

It says that He became sin. He didn't just take care of my behavior; He *became* my behavior. You need to catch this! So if I'm behaving wrongly, then I haven't realized what He's done, and therefore I haven't matured into the identity of who He says I am. When my behavior is continually immature, it's because I haven't come to (or through) the innocence of being matured so I can be reconciled to God.

Walking in Innocence

After the conference, I started to get texts from Randy. He said, "I'm sorry about when we went to lunch. I didn't act innocent."

I replied, "Yeah, but I declared you innocent."

He sent back, "But I didn't behave innocently."

When we had gone to lunch he had said, "Man, God revealed to me that He had told you to spiritually murder me." After I confirmed that, Randy had said, "And you're good at it too!"

I had replied, "Oh, yeah. But I had to spiritually murder you because you wouldn't judge yourself."

LEARNING THE MECHANICS OF INNOCENCE

> Put to death therefore what is earthly in you: sexual immorality, impurity, passion, evil desire and covetousness, which is idolatry (Colossians 3:5).

The same verse in the King James Version says you "mortify" the deeds of the flesh.

One key is that you have to stop looking for Jesus to do something that He's already done. Because you're innocent, you can mortify your behavior and bring it into alignment under the power of the Holy Spirit to walk in holiness, purity, and righteousness.

Randy also shared that he had seen some people at the conference who used to be under his leadership and that he didn't act innocent toward them. I said, "Well, you're probably not innocent to them yet. They're still walking through their issues, just like we are. They heard the message too!" We are still figuring out the mechanics of how innocence works, but God said that if we start with a verbal decree of innocence, grace will follow.

If your prayer requests start off with all your failures, then you have put yourself in the wrong position. Here is a prayer in proper alignment: "Father, I know You made me innocent, but my behavior doesn't line up to that truth. Please reveal my false identity, where I have not matured into Your likeness and grace. Show me, because my behavior is not coinciding with the foundation of unstained innocence." That is my new prayer.

The Kissing Prophet

All that with Randy happened on Friday, but the whole weekend messed me up—totally messed me up. As I walked into the Saturday session, Leif Hetland was preaching about the Father's love. Leif is anointed for this message. He has gone to Pakistan and other parts of the Muslim world for the last twenty-five years and kisses Muslims to release the Father's love over them. They call him "the apostle of love." He's one of our spiritual brothers in the Jack Taylor family.

THE BAPTISM OF INNOCENCE

As Leif was finishing his message about the Father's love, he looked directly at Randy and made a beeline for him. Leif laid hands on Randy and gave him a kiss, and Randy was covered with the Father's love and fell under the power of that love. It broke something on the inside of Randy.

I felt the Holy Spirit stirring on the inside of me and I went into a vision where I saw that Leif is called to release the Father's love to God's people and the world at large. God showed me that the greatest move of God is being released, and it's the love of the Father that will change the world. In that vision I also saw many church-going people who are unable to receive the Father's love.

As the vision continued, the Lord showed me that the "baptism of innocence" would be released to the body of Christ so that God's people would stop stiff-arming God the Father when He tried to love them. So many of us have stiff-armed the Father because we don't think we are innocent enough to receive His love. Still in the vision, I saw myself kissing people and declaring their innocence. Until you understand your innocence, you will never position yourself for the Father's love because you don't think you're worthy to receive it.

I'm telling you, I never thought I'd be a kissing prophet! As I started putting the mechanics of innocence as a principle to work in my life, the Lord started opening up the Scriptures to the foundational truth of the gospel.

The Next Generation of Prophets

I came into Saturday night's meeting, and one of the senior leaders, Lisa, was holding a little baby. I knew it wasn't hers; she was holding a baby that belonged to somebody else in the congregation. But the Lord said to me, "She's taking care of the baby, but she's a warrior worshiper. I need her to do some warfare, so you need to hold the baby."

I replied to the Lord, "I don't... do babies." But I offered to take the baby.

LEARNING THE MECHANICS OF INNOCENCE

Lisa looked at me with that "are you sure" look as she handed the baby over to me.

"Yes, I'm fine," I replied. "I will not drop the kid!"

Then she started worshiping, and the power of God was just running through the place.

Meanwhile, I was holding the baby and the Lord said to me, "Until the prophets start taking care of the babies, the babies will never grow up to be prophets." The Lord continued, "Look at his face. Isn't he innocent? You're holding a prophet. He's just in baby form, but until the prophets take care of the babies, they'll never mature into prophets. But the babies must understand their innocence before they'll ever become strong prophets. And they're only going to learn by your example."

It felt like hours while I held this baby. People were seeing a sign and a wonder! I found out that the baby belonged to a couple who were in leadership at the church, Sean and Alden. I had previously prophesied over his mother when he was in her womb that he would be a prophet to the nations. I didn't know whose baby it was when I grabbed him.

God is saying, "In the next generation, I will raise up a company of innocent prophets who will speak with purity and clarity. But many of My prophets who don't understand innocence will always lean to the mean side of the prophetic. They will always go to wrath.

When He said that, my reaction was, "That's me. I'm guilty as charged!" When we go to judgment first, it's because we don't understand innocence or the power of the finished work of the cross. We find the negative so quick because we don't have an identity of innocence. God is looking for a people who can release His grace and release His mercy. But the first thing we need to do is be baptized in innocence.

Discipline, not Punishment

The following Sunday, a lady in the parking lot came up to me, saying, "Are you the pastor?" When I confirmed that I was, she asked,

THE BAPTISM OF INNOCENCE

"Will you pray for me? My son is an addict. He's destroying my house. My husband wants to leave me because of this."

I asked the woman, "Why would you let your son destroy your home?" His behavior was destroying her home and her marriage. She was allowing his behavior to do that.

I offered, "Give him the option to get healed and change his behavior." As I said it, I was thinking, *I'm giving her this advice; how does that line up with innocence?*

We think innocence is a license to misbehave, but it's not. It's an opportunity to bring maturity. With innocence as a foundation, we start being molded into the image of Jesus. When you're innocent, it means you're coming to Him like a child, and children need discipline, not punishment. Religion punishes you because you weren't worthy. Religion says, "Oh, you're a dirty dog. You don't measure up." But that's just the devil talking. Jesus says, "You're innocent, you're pure, you're Holy, you're Mine." Then when He brings correction, it's not punishment, it's *discipline*. The Father says, "Son, I made you innocent; now act like it."

> And have you forgotten his encouraging words spoken to you as his children? He said, "My child, don't underestimate the value of the discipline and training of the Lord God, or get depressed when he has to correct you." For the Lord's training of your life is evidence of his faithful love. And when he draws you to himself, it proves you are his delightful child. Fully embrace God's correction as part of your training, for he is doing what any loving father does for his children. For who has ever heard of a child who never had to be corrected? We all should welcome God's discipline as a validation of authentic sonship. For if we have never once endured his correction it only proves we are strangers and not sons. And isn't it true that we respect our earthly fathers even though they corrected and disciplined us? Then we should demonstrate an even greater respect for

LEARNING THE MECHANICS OF INNOCENCE

God, our spiritual Father, as we submit to his life-giving discipline (Hebrews 12:5–9 TPT).

As I held that baby for what felt like hours, it was interesting that the Lord was making my heart more tender and my spirit teachable. As the weekend of that conference ended, I drove to my friend's home, who is the prophet in the leadership of the ministry. When I got out of the car, their big dog bit me—even drawing blood on my left hand. They were freaking out because of it. But I heard the Lord instruct me not to overreact about it.

I asked God what revelation He was going to give me over the dog biting me. I knew that the whole conference was a life-changing weekend for me and that God was continuing His explanation of what was about to come on the earth.

Late that night as I got ready for bed, God told me this, "There will be those who will not accept the innocence message, and they will bite you like a dog. But when they draw blood as you walk in innocence, it will be My blood of innocence that will flow."

I asked Him, "Are You telling me that they're going to bite me?"

He replied, "Yes, they are. They're going to wrestle with you, they're going to debate with you, and they will attack this message and your character." He continued to instruct, "Do not overreact or you will put undue shame on those who need the baptism of innocence the most. Let the dogs bite. When they bite an innocent man and he doesn't react, they will be bitten by My love and then I can heal them."

He could have spoken that to me in a dream rather than an actual dog bite! But I know now that when it hits, it will hurt! We will need His grace.

***

Wisdom Keys:

1. The baptism of innocence gives you the ability to resist demonic attractions.
2. The baptism of innocence stops us from stiff-arming the Father when He is trying to love us.
3. The baptism of innocence transforms punishment into loving discipline and true sonship.
4. People with a religious spirit will bite you like a dog.

Chapter 3: The Foundation of Innocence Is Love

If love is the foundation on which innocence has to be built, we must take a deeper look into love. But that foundation of love has to be revealed in our hearts before we realize that He has made us innocent. If love is the foundation, then we must inspect that truth and see if we have a true understanding of who love is, how love is accessed, and what the perfecting process looks like.

> By this we know that we abide in him and he in us, because he has given us of his Spirit. And we have seen and testify that the Father has sent his Son to be the Savior of the world (1 John 4:13–14).

The Cross Is Love

The starting point is the fact that abiding in Christ by the Spirit is the process of making love your foundation. You must recognize that the Father sent Jesus to save the world because of His love for mankind, so the finished work of the cross is love at its foundation. As brutal and humiliating as it was, if the foundation of the crucifixion was not love, it would have been sadistic, to say the least. The power behind the cross is that Jesus was a man without sin. He was innocent and still was crucified for us to be reconciled with the Father. The principle of "you can't give away what you don't have" even applies to Jesus; having that understanding and belief that He was innocent is a must.

THE BAPTISM OF INNOCENCE

> For we do not have a high priest who is unable to sympathize with our weaknesses, but one who in every respect has been tempted as we are, yet without sin (Hebrews 4:15).

The sinless Jesus has to be a reality in your heart because when the baptism of innocence is poured on you, that truth will become a reality in your heart, and "as [a man] thinks in his heart, so is he" (Proverbs 23:7 NKJV). The fact of this belief is a major part of the revelation process in which we can be transformed into the image of Christ, who was sinless and innocent.

> Whoever confesses that Jesus is the Son of God, God abides in him, and he in God. So we have come to know and to believe the love that God has for us. God is love, and whoever abides in love abides in God, and God abides in him. By this is love perfected with us, so that we may have confidence for the day of judgment, because as he is so also are we in this world (1 John 4:15–17).

The confession from your heart that Jesus was sinless and abiding within the Godhead is the connection to the source of love and innocence. When it is tapped into through relationships of life, it starts to become self-multiplying in nature. The more we abide, the more we pull the energy of love from the Father, and the power of the Holy Spirit comes into play—and we walk through life's issues and form the mental passages within our emotions that will pull from love and filter through a understanding of innocence. This will become a natural process as we become perfected in love.

> There is no fear in love, but perfect love casts out fear. For fear has to do with punishment, and whoever fears has not been perfected in love. We love because he first loved us (1 John 4:18–19).

This part of love has been very difficult for me personally to overcome. I was introduced to Jesus in a time that Susie and I were in the process of a divorce; and I was still addicted to porn, and I had other

THE FOUNDATION OF INNOCENCE IS LOVE

character flaws that made me tell God that His promise of healing my marriage would not work because I was a cheater at the core and I could not be trusted. After the Lord dealt with me about the promise of my marriage and family restoration, I came to the fact that I would cheat if presented with the right situation. Maybe not for months or even years, but in time if the situation was presented, I would cheat. This was the truth about me. The Lord had given me a true agape love for Susie and I never wanted to hurt her again. At this point, I asked to be released from the promise of healing my marriage so Susie could find a husband that would never hurt her again in that area.

The Lord had a different plan and started a three-day debate with me about asking to be released from the promises. On the third day, at 2:30 in the afternoon, the Lord asked if He guaranteed me that I would never touch another woman in an inappropriate way, would I still want to be released from the promise of healing my marriage? I asked, "Can you guarantee that?" He spoke sternly, saying, "I AM God."

I thought for a minute and said, "If you can guarantee that, yes—I want you to heal my marriage." With that agreement, the Lord told me to get up and stand on my Bible. As I stood on my Bible, the Lord spoke audibly with a voice like thunder and said, "Charles Layton Coker Jr., if you ever touch another woman in an inappropriate manner, I will *kill you stone dead.*" Well, that took care of that issue in a New York minute—it was done!

I know the Scriptures say, "The fear of the Lord is the beginning of wisdom, and the knowledge of the Holy One is insight" (Proverbs 9:10).

I know that this is a reverential fear and not the fear that the enemy uses to torment and punish. But within this process, the fear from the enemy took root within me, and I became dogmatic in my walk with the Lord. I developed a heart that was very legalistic in nature and therefore love and innocence had no foundation to grow from. For over seven years, I would not hug a woman for fear that I may enter into lust and get zapped by God. As I walked out this process of being perfected by love, I found that I was a racist and had a history from being wounded by some black leaders in school, and the enemy used that wound to develop a prejudiced mindset. The Lord dealt with that in a very short order. That's a different topic in and of itself. The spirit of racism isn't racist; it's demonic!

> If anyone says, "I love God," and hates his brother, he is a liar; for he who does not love his brother whom he has seen cannot love God whom he has not seen. And this commandment we have from him: whoever loves God must also love his brother (1 John 4:20–21).

If you believe that God is love and that He has taken residence inside of you, it is impossible to hate your brother and love God at the same time and be at peace. The only way is to walk in a twisted belief of what love is. The God-kind of love we are talking about is *agape*, "unconditional God-love." When you mix your understanding of who God is with the different kinds of love, you will get a twisted view and not be able to walk in innocence.

Four Types of Love

When it comes to love, the Bible has a lot to say about it. To get a good handle on what we need to know about love and how it relates to innocence, I want to differentiate all of these types of love from a biblical standpoint.

We all know that God is love, so it should not surprise us that God talks about it a lot. But our English word *love* is very inadequate when it comes to the meaning behind what God communicated about it in Scripture. In fact, there are four main Greek words found in the New Testament with vastly different meanings for what we know as love. These words are *storge*, *philos*, *eros*, and *agape*. Let's take a closer look at each of these.

Storge—Familial Love

Storge (pronounced *STOR-jay*) is a Greek term that describes affection within a family. It is the bond that happens naturally between parents and their children, brothers and sisters, and other types of family relationships. The Bible is full of examples of this type of familial love, from the relationship that Jacob had with his sons, to Mary, Martha and Lazarus in the New Testament.

Though not found directly in Scripture itself, Romans chapter 12 has an interesting compound word that includes *storge*. The word is *philostorgos* and speaks about brotherly affection:

> Let love be genuine. Abhor what is evil; hold fast to what is good. Love one another with brotherly affection. Outdo one another in showing honor (Romans 12:9–10).

Philos—Friendship Love

Philos (pronounced *FEE-los*) is the bond of friendship that we see among Christians. It is the love one has for someone who is not a family member. Jesus used this word when He said that this type of friendship was the best kind you can have for another:

> Greater love has no one than this, that someone lay down his life for his friends (John 15:13).

And just a few verses later Jesus called us His *philos*, His friends:

> No longer do I call you servants, for the servant does not know what his master is doing; but I have called you friends, for all that I have heard from my Father I have made known to you (John 15:15).

It was also this type of friendship God declared to have with Abraham because he chose to believe God:

> And the Scripture was fulfilled that says, "Abraham believed God, and it was counted to him as righteousness"—and he was called a friend of God (James 2:23).

THE BAPTISM OF INNOCENCE

Eros—Romantic Love

Eros (pronounced *AIR-ohs*) is the Greek word for romantic love between a man and woman. The term came from the mythological Greek god of love and sexual desire. There are no instances of *eros* found in Scripture, but we see the early church fighting the cultural promiscuity that was rampant in ancient Greek culture. Paul's letters to the Corinthian church got very direct sometimes as he had to deal with situations where love was being polluted in the church and was no longer pure.

> Flee from sexual immorality. Every other sin a person commits is outside the body, but the sexually immoral person sins against his own body (1 Cor. 6:18).

Paul also addressed the Ephesian believers, warning them that those who are sexually immoral should be removed from the church so they did not influence others. It is interesting to note that he tells them to walk in *agape* love toward each other.

> Therefore be imitators of God, as beloved children. And walk in love, as Christ loved us and gave himself up for us, a fragrant offering and sacrifice to God. But sexual immorality and all impurity or covetousness must not even be named among you, as is proper among saints (Eph. 5:1–3).

Our society today isn't so different than it was in the early church. We all deal with a barrage of sexual immorality trying to constantly sway us from our innocence.

Agape—Unconditional "God" Love

Agape (Pronounced *uh-GAH-pay*): This is the highest form of love that can be found in the Bible. It encompasses the great unconditional love that God has for all humanity. This Greek word is found over a hundred times in the New Testament. It is this type of love that sent Jesus to the cross.

> But God shows his love for us in that while we were still sinners, Christ died for us (Romans 5:8).

Jesus declared that having this type of love for others would be a testimony to everyone that we belong to Him:

> By this all people will know that you are my disciples, if you have love for one another (John 13:35).

And it is this *agape* love that Romans chapter 8 declares that we can never be separated from:

> Who shall separate us from the love of Christ? Shall tribulation, or distress, or persecution, or famine, or nakedness, or danger, or sword?… For I am sure that neither death nor life, nor angels nor rulers, nor things present nor things to come, nor powers, nor height nor depth, nor anything else in all creation, will be able to separate us from the love of God in Christ Jesus our Lord (Romans 8:35, 38–39).

There is a story in John chapter 21 that takes place after Jesus's resurrection and before he was taken up to heaven. Before Jesus's crucifixion, Peter had not only denied that he knew Jesus, he even swore about it. To Peter, theirs was a broken relationship; he had failed miserably. On the heels of that memory, Jesus comes back around to Peter to bring restoration.

> When they had finished breakfast, Jesus said to Simon Peter, "Simon, son of John, do you love me more than these?" He said to him, "Yes, Lord; you know that I love you." He said to him, "Feed my lambs." He said to him a second time, "Simon, son of John, do you love me?" He said to him, "Yes, Lord; you know that I love you." He said to him, "Tend my sheep." He said to him the third time, "Simon, son of John, do you love me?" Peter was grieved because he said to him the third time, "Do you love me?" and he said

to him, "Lord, you know everything; you know that I love you." Jesus said to him, "Feed my sheep" (John 21:15–17).

It is interesting to note that the first two times Jesus asked Peter if he loved Him, Jesus used the word *agape*, and both times, Peter responded with the word *phileo*, which has its root in *philos*. Jesus was asking Peter if he loved Him dearly, to which Peter basically replied, "Yes, Jesus, You're my friend; You know I like you." So the third time around, if we look at the Greek words, we see that Jesus switched His question to use the word to *phileo*. This is what elicits the response that we see from Peter and why he was so grieved about it. Jesus met Peter right where he was at in order to restore Him in the love of God. Jesus lowered His expectation for Peter to grow into *agape* and not leave him on *phileo*.

Agape: The Foundational Love

Agape love is the DNA of God Himself, and all other forms of love build from this *agape* foundation. When a mother has the *agape* love of God as her foundation, her *storge* love will have balance and maturing principles.

This works the same with *philos* love. When the DNA of *agape* is the foundation your friendship, brotherly love will be encouraging and safe. Do you remember what Cain asked when he got into trouble with God about what happened to his brother, Abel? Cain's wrong answer was, "Am I my brother's keeper?" The reason God got so upset with Cain was because he didn't have *agape* or *philos* love for his brother. I believe that when true *agape* love is poured on us with the baptism of innocence, the body of Christ will start to reflect the brotherly love that attracts the world to see Jesus through us all according to the following verse:

> A new commandment I give to you, that you love one another: just as I have loved you, you also are to love one another. By this all people will know that you are my disciples, if you have love for one another (John 13:34–35).

When *eros* has its foundation built on *agape*, our sexuality will become pure and healthy. When our relationships become broken or nonexistent, the result is a complete breakdown in marriage, which opens the door for the enemy to destroy us. I am very adamant about keeping a balance in this area because of my broken past being a porn addict, which completely destroyed my marriage. It took years after I was saved for my wife to recover because I was broken and did not have *agape* as my foundation, nor did I walk in the baptism of innocence. I have seen *eros* preached as love with a hook in it. That's a great description of romantic love outside of a marriage covenant. Young people can explain the drive of *eros* better than anyone else when their hormones start kicking in.

> Honor the sanctity of marriage and keep your vows of purity to one another, for God will judge sexual immorality in any form, whether single or married (Hebrews 13:4 TPT).

Innocence Leads to Holiness

When *eros* is in balance with the baptism of innocence, there is a purity and satisfaction that is truly heavenly. The baptism of innocence brings unconditional love that holds no record of wrong and allows us to walk in holiness and purity with power—then it becomes a weapon that the enemy has to flee from.

> And was declared to be the Son of God in power according to the Spirit of holiness by his resurrection from the dead, Jesus Christ our Lord (Romans 1:4).

This was part of the Apostle Paul's résumé to the Roman church. Without the resurrection, you are not innocent. When the finished work of the cross and resurrection was completed, you became innocent—and when you are innocent, you can walk in holiness.

Holiness is being led by the Spirit. The Holy Spirit says, "Okay, this habit isn't going to send you to hell, but I wish you wouldn't act that way." The Spirit gives us the grace to be empowered to walk it out.

THE BAPTISM OF INNOCENCE

> By purity, knowledge, patience, kindness, the Holy Spirit, genuine love; by truthful speech, and the power of God; with the weapons of righteousness for the right hand and for the left (2 Cor. 6:6–7).

Purity was an attribute of God that I considered to be a weapon because I didn't understand my innocence. Yet innocence is the very thing that allows me to walk in purity and holiness. I had been duped on the religious hamster wheel of performance, and I had given up my innocence. But for innocence to become a weapon of warfare, you have to confront the lies of the enemy with the truth that you are innocent. When the devil starts coming at you with the mistakes of your past, you need to remind yourself and the devil that you are innocent because of the finished work of the cross.

You are innocent! You are not guilty, which means there wasn't enough evidence to convict you of the crime or put you in jail.

> For our sake he made him to be sin who knew no sin, so that in him we might become the righteousness of God (2 Cor. 5:21).

> The Spirit of the Lord is upon me, because he has anointed me to proclaim good news to the poor. He has sent me to proclaim liberty to the captives and recovering of sight to the blind, to set at liberty those who are oppressed, to proclaim the year of the Lord's favor (Luke 4:18–19).

When Jesus says He became my sin in 2 Corinthians 5:21, it reveals the reason that the anointing was on Jesus in Luke 4:18. When you break it down, it says, "The Spirit of the Lord is upon me to set the prisoner and the captive free." The captive and the prisoner. Listen, the prisoner deserves to be in prison. A captive was put there because of somebody else's behavior or sin—but He sets both free.

There are things that you've done that the devil says you deserve to be punished for, but Jesus says, "No, I became sin and the behavior from sin for them. They are set free." Jesus is not a loophole. When we treat Him as our loophole, then we have to jump through the "hoop-hole" of performance. Do unto others as God has done unto you: Forgive them of their sins and set both the prisoner and the captive free.

Think about this: If He is in you, and you are in Him, then where are you seated according to John 14:20, which says, "In that day you will know that I am in my Father, and you in me, and I in you?" On the throne! You're not looking at the throne; you are on the throne with Christ.

Look at yourself in the mirror and declare that you are innocent. Say this: "I'm innocent. Not guilty wasn't good enough; I'm innocent." It starts with each of us personally. In the next season, we have to quit looking for a baptism of love and start looking for baptism of innocence. Then love will follow right behind it. Innocence will rebuild a faulty foundation and help return to love properly.

You might be thinking, *If I'm innocent, then why am I always wrestling with generational curses? If I'm really innocent, they shouldn't exist.* Realize that it's a mindset. The enemy has been tormenting Christians to go after generational curses that Jesus has already cancelled. That's right! Jesus already cancelled them; you don't have to work as hard as you thought you did.

Now think about this: If you're in Christ, where did the generational curses go? They're gone! I know who my parents were and I know their lifestyles before they received Christ, and let me tell you that they had some generational curses. Not knowing this revelation had me go after our family curses because I was living on the wrong side of the cross. But when I get on the other side of the finished work of the cross and declare my lineage as innocent, the sins of the fathers that have tried to torment me will vanish as I declare them of no effect. Because of that, I can walk in the purity and holiness of my family line that goes back to Jesus Himself, back to Adam, and ultimately back to the Father. Why? Because He reconciled us in Christ.

> Therefore, if anyone is in Christ, he is a new creation. The old has passed away; behold, the new has come. All this is

> from God, who through Christ reconciled us to himself and gave us the ministry of reconciliation (2 Cor. 5:17–18).

All this is from God, who reconciled us to himself through Christ and gave us the ministry of reconciliation. Come on, Jesus!

Getting Rid of Justification

When the baptism of innocence comes, you gain the ability to see the feet of clay on a person and still find the gold on the inside of them. I believe more than anything that you will have a false identity without the revelation of innocence. I named our church "Identity Church," knowing that identity is the key to the abundant life in Christ, and we cannot function properly in our relationships with God and our relationships with those around us if we have a false identity. And if our identity with God is missing the DNA of innocence, we have a false identity. Therefore, our behavior will not line up to the truth of who we are in Christ.

I found that I didn't know what the ministry of reconciliation really looked like, so I didn't know how to apply it. The Lord made this statement to me: "Most of my children don't know what it looks like to enter into the ministry of reconciliation because they continue to have conversations of justification." Having conversations of justification is not innocence; it's a false identity. But the Father is about to kiss His people with the baptism of innocence, and we've got to get this settled so that the kiss from the Father will have its effect of empowering and winning the world with His love.

A few weeks after I preached on the baptism of innocence, a lady contacted me to give her testimony. She said during the conference, I had kissed her on the cheek and declared her innocent. I had given instructions to let innocence finish its work and destroy the paperwork she had on herself first. This woman's husband had cheated on her in 2005, and though she said she had forgiven him, there was still paperwork. When she declared him innocent, it changed their marriage in a supernatural way.

THE FOUNDATION OF INNOCENCE IS LOVE

If we keep looking at our behavior and the behavior of others and saying, "That's not innocence," then we're not letting God do His completed work in us, making us as innocent as a child, which brings us into maturity and Christlikeness.

***

Wisdom Keys:

1. Even Jesus had to be innocent before He could give it away.
2. The four kinds of love will be twisted if the foundational love is not agape (the DNA of God).
3. The revelation of your innocence will keep you from a false identity.

Chapter 4: Forgiven

In our quest to understand what it is like to live on the other side of the cross, we have to compare the old and new covenants. It really is a matter of life and death to be sure of what covenant you are focusing on. There is a great difference between which covenant you pull the life-giving power from. If you are not pulling the Holy Spirit into your life after the crucifixion and resurrection, you will have a tainted view with a false identity. It's Law versus grace. Trust me, you cannot get to the baptism of innocence with the wrong side of the cross theology. The Law is very clear that nobody can obtain innocence while they are under its authority. Thank God, the finished work of the cross and resurrection fulfilled the requirement of the Law.

Look what Romans 3:19–20 tells us. I love *The Passion Translation* in this verse.

> Now, we realize that everything the law says is addressed to those who are under its authority. This is for two reasons: So that every excuse will be silenced, with no boasting of innocence. And so that the entire world will be held accountable to God's standards or by the merit of observing the law no one earns the status of being declared righteous before God, for it is the law that fully exposes and unmasks the reality of sin.

I'm so glad that we don't live under the law. The verses above show that it's the power on the other side of the cross that gives us the ability in Christ to be innocent.

THE BAPTISM OF INNOCENCE

I love looking in the Old Testament to find the promises of the Father to see what the finished work of the cross is going to look like. Isaiah 42:6 is one of those verses:

> I am the Lord; I have called you in righteousness; I will take you by the hand and keep you; I will give you as a covenant for the people, a light for the nations.

Just remember—Jesus was called the Light and Life, and now more than ever, the nations need some fresh Light and new Life!

> Now before faith came, we were held captive under the law, imprisoned until the coming faith would be revealed. So then, the law was our guardian until Christ came, in order that we might be justified by faith. But now that faith has come, we are no longer under a guardian, for in Christ Jesus you are all sons of God, through faith. For as many of you as were baptized into Christ have put on Christ (Gal. 3:23–27).

The cross is where Jesus Christ made atonement for our sins. Because of Christ's death on the cross, I was forgiven of all my sins. The Lamb who knew no sin became my sin, and was the complete sacrifice that fulfilled the requirements of the Law. Nobody can come to salvation without believing that Jesus completed the work of redemption on the cross.

Not only does the act of the cross give me forgiveness of sin, it also gives me expiation of sin. *Expiation* means to clear away the record, to make it as if it never existed—and it is not something you can do for yourself. It's part of the total package of redemption.

When I was first born again, I was told the story that sounded good, but it wasn't true. It went something like this: When I sinned, there was a video in heaven where the devil showed Jesus and the Father that I had committed a sin. As he played the video, Jesus stood up and told all of heaven that I covered this with His blood. Then the video goes blank with a red screen, because the blood of Jesus had covered my sin.

The next level of the cross is *propitiation*. The cross didn't just take my sin or punishment away. Jesus *became* my sin. The One who knew no sin became sin on my behalf.

> For our sake he made him to be sin who knew no sin, so that in him we might become the righteousness of God (2 Cor. 5:21).

> He is the propitiation for our sins, and not for ours only but also for the sins of the whole world (1 John 2:2).

One Drop of Blood

I am reminded of an encounter I had when I was first saved that transformed my understanding of the cross and what it accomplished for me.

I had a vision in which I was sitting and weeping as I hugged the bottom of the cross with Jesus hanging on it.

As I looked up at Him, He looked down at me and His eyes seemed to look right through me. They were screaming, "I LOVE YOU!" Then He died. I saw that His side had been pierced with a spear, and the angle of the wound was as though it was cut from bottom up, and blood and water were pouring out of His side. As I looked closer, there was a stream of blood leaking from the opening on the bottom part of the wound, and it looked like thick, pure blood rather than being mixed with water. It was running down the length of His torso and down the outside of His thighs. His legs were crossed with one foot was on top of the other, one nail piercing both feet, which caused the blood to move from the side of His thighs to the front. Then the stream of blood moved and ran down over the top of the knee, down the length of His shin, down to the front of His foot, past the nail, and came to His big toe. As I looked up, I saw the blood pool up and cover His whole big toe. Then I saw a drop of blood leave His toe, my eyes were fixed on this drop of blood, as I followed it, I felt it land on the top of my head.

THE BAPTISM OF INNOCENCE

Immediately, peace covered my soul. I instantly found an internal harmony in my mind and divine rest for my soul. This is what total forgiveness for all your sins feels like! I had a peaceful bliss run through my veins and my spirit man came alive with the understanding of how much the Father loved me, and how much Jesus loved me to endure the horrific pain of the crucifixion.

> Therefore, since we are surrounded by so great a cloud of witnesses, let us also lay aside every weight, and sin which clings so closely, and let us run with endurance the race that is set before us, looking to Jesus, the founder and perfecter of our faith, who for the joy that was set before him endured the cross, despising the shame, and is seated at the right hand of the throne of God (Heb. 12:1–2).

The revelation in this encounter progresses through three different levels: forgiveness, shame, and innocence. We will start with the level of forgiveness.

Proving Forgiveness

Naturally, we start with the forgiveness of sins. The weight of my sin had become unbearable, and I was unable to carry them any longer. What an amazing sensation to have sin removed from my innermost being! I finally found peace in my spirit; my soul and mind were finally at peace. Not only was my mind at peace from the torment, but it had been renewed with an understanding of who God was, and how much He loved me. One drop of His blood cleaned my soul and supernaturally removed a sin-consciousness—a complete "big-bang theory," if you will. The scripture I have repeated several times in this book became reality to me. He became my sin, and it was removed. My sin was finally forgiven, but living life in such a way that I had no unforgiveness in my heart toward others was more difficult to accomplish. It's just like when God asked me to prove that I had received innocence by declaring Randy innocent—it's where the rubber meets the road.

FORGIVEN

Proving that you have been forgiven of your sin becomes real when you forgive others of their sins. That's where the real power lies. Let's look back to the first encounter Jesus had with His disciples after His resurrection in John chapter 20:

> Jesus said to them again, "Peace be with you. As the Father has sent me, even so I am sending you." And when he had said this, he breathed on them and said to them, "Receive the Holy Spirit. If you forgive the sins of any, they are forgiven them; if you withhold forgiveness from any, it is withheld" (John 20:21–23).

Forgiving others is how we prove that we have received forgiveness. When you choose not to, it initiates a lifestyle that is not based on the finished work of the cross. Let's look at what Jesus has to say about unforgiveness and bitterness, a heart condition cultivated from not forgiving others. Peace is a good indicator of if total forgiveness has been completed or not. Here is a wisdom key that I use to remind me of this truth: "If my peace has left, I am not right."

> Then said he unto the disciples, It is impossible but that offences will come: but woe *unto him*, through whom they come! It were better for him that a millstone were hanged about his neck, and he cast into the sea, than that he should offend one of these little ones. Take heed to yourselves: If thy brother trespass against thee, rebuke him; and if he repent, forgive him. And if he trespass against thee seven times in a day, and seven times in a day turn again to thee, saying, I repent; thou shalt forgive him (Luke 17:1–4 KJV, emphasis mine).

Jesus said that you can expect offences to come into your life at some point, and when they do, they will test your ability to forgive. It *will* happen! Trust me, Susie and I have been married for over forty years. THEY WILL COME! We have also been in business and pastoring a church—and we know that is true in those areas too: THEY WILL COME!

Have Some Faith

But Jesus doesn't stop there, He tells us if someone repents, we have to forgive them—even if they are some kind of repeat offender psycho and we have to do it seven times a day. If this is the proof that Jesus forgave me of all my sins, I can't do it. But if He became my sin, I can only prove it by a supernatural ability that only God can give. That's why the apostles asked the Lord to increase their faith in Luke chapter 17:

> And the apostles said unto the Lord, Increase our faith. And the Lord said, If ye had faith as a grain of mustard seed, ye might say unto this sycamine tree, Be thou plucked up by the root, and be thou planted in the sea; and it should obey you (Luke 17:5–6 KJV).

In response to their request, Jesus gave an example of how unforgiveness will kill you on the inside and how it can be dealt with by faith through the finished work of the cross.

I can picture Jesus sitting under a huge sycamine tree, similar to the one in the picture below, while telling them this parable. This tree represents bitterness and unforgiveness!

Jesus was telling this story about what bitterness and unforgiveness will do to a person who allows unforgiveness of others in their life. Remember that He is telling them this before the finished work of the cross. He told them that by faith they could pluck up a sycamine tree by the roots and throw it in to the sea. This is a blueprint of what the finished work of the cross gives us.

Sycamine trees are very common throughout the Middle East. They are also known as sycamore fig trees, and they have very unusual characteristics. It is a very large tree which has a deep root system. Its roots go deep, which makes it hard to kill, but also gives it the ability to live in dry places with very little water. It was the preferred wood to build caskets. It is interesting to find out that this tree is only pollinated by wasps stinging the heart of the fruit. And the fruit that is produced looks like the fig of a Mulberry tree, but it is so bitter that you can only nibble on it a little at a time.

So by faith we can pull out the deep roots of unforgiveness, have peace, and stop nibbling on the fruit of the records of wrongs that people have done to us. We can stop building the casket of death in our lives, and start living from the water of the Spirit again. When the finished work of the cross becomes reality to us, we will be able to go beyond just being forgiven of our sins, and we can begin releasing that forgiveness to others.

Unforgiveness Blocks the Power

In Mark 11, we find a parable about mountain-moving power being blocked by unforgiveness.

> Truly, I say to you, whoever says to this mountain, "Be taken up and thrown into the sea," and does not doubt in his heart, but believes that what he says will come to pass, it will be done for him. Therefore I tell you, whatever you ask in prayer, believe that you have received it, and it will be yours. And whenever you stand praying, forgive, if you have anything against anyone, so that your Father also who is in heaven may forgive you your trespasses (Mark 11:23–25).

If we have unforgiveness in our heart, the mountain-moving power that the Word promises can and will be hindered. Doubt and unbelief are grown in the soil of unforgiveness. Our lack of power is linked to unforgiveness between us and our fellow man.

THE BAPTISM OF INNOCENCE

Just remember that the finished work of the cross had not been provided by Jesus at this time. So only after the death, burial, and resurrection did He breathe on the disciples and give these instructions about forgiveness.

Years ago, I asked the Lord to give me a wisdom key about forgiveness. He said, *"Biblical forgiveness is a verbal request with a physical willingness to restore or repay."*

So this mountain-moving power is voice activated. You have to be verbal when a relationship is being repaired. First, you have to be verbal with yourself and God, and then after you have dealt with yourself and the paperwork (record of wrongs) that you hold in your heart, you need to be willing to speak to whomever needs to hear it and be given the same opportunity. Forgiveness has to be applied first before the baptism of innocence can finish the restoration of a relationship. Openly speaking with your brother is part of the physical aspect of releasing the baptism of innocence to others. This is proof that you are walking in it.

Bringing Restoration

Willingness to restore is where the rubber meets the road. Restoring relationships is hard because trust has been broken, feelings have been hurt, and pride will get in the way.

I have seen the supernatural working of the baptism of innocence in relational restoration, and that relationship becomes stronger than it was before the offence happened. There normally is an additional release of gratitude on both parties that come into their hearts. I consider it to be one of the mysteries of the kingdom. It's also one of the commanded blessings listed in Psalms 133.

> Behold, how good and pleasant it is when brothers dwell in unity! It is like the precious oil on the head, running down on the beard, on the beard of Aaron, running down on the collar of his robes! It is like the dew of Hermon, which falls on the mountains of Zion! For there the Lord has commanded the blessing, life forevermore (Psalm 133).

What about the part of repaying? If a man steals my car and then gets convicted from the Lord to ask me for forgiveness for stealing the car, I would have to forgive him of stealing my car. But I would also expect him to return the car to me. So if we forgive someone for an offence that broke the relationship, we have to be willing to also restore the relationship, not just say, "I forgive you," and never speak to them again. That is not the ministry of reconciliation that Jesus is talking about.

This baptism of innocence is a vital part that takes us through the next stages to the finished work of the cross, which starts with the understanding that Jesus became our sin and forgave us. But we still have to learn a lot about shame, innocence, and then childlikeness. We will be getting into each of these areas through the rest of the book.

**

Wisdom Keys:

1. The "wrong side of the cross" theology will keep you from the baptism of innocence.
2. Forgiving others is proof that we have received forgiveness.
3. Doubt and unbelief are grown in the soil of unforgiveness.
4. Mountain-moving power is voice-activated.

Chapter 5: Shamelessness and Innocence

Many times while preaching throughout the country, I've told the story of the encounter with Jesus on the cross and how the drop of blood dripped from His toe and cleaned my mind and soul, and how that one drop of His innocent blood changed my life. But there was something stirring in my spirit about that encounter.

I had just finished writing a book about me and Susie's journey called *From Rape to Righteousness: Redeeming the Bride of Christ*, and openly wrote about how I was raped at knifepoint when I was seven years old by a man who died on death row. In that book, I also share how I raped and abused Susie at fifteen years old—just like the saying goes, hurt people, hurt people. Writing that book required me to be the most vulnerable I have ever been. It took me some time to deal with my own emotions, and even some pain from my past that was still a residue in my heart. One of the people who endorsed my book had a conversation with me about how I dealt with the shame from my past. So I shared privately a very personal part of the encounter that I had never shared publicly.

After the drop of blood left Jesus's toe and landed on the top of my head, transforming my spirit, renewing my mind, and showing how much Jesus loved me, the Lord said something very personal to me. He said, "Did you notice that I was a circumcised Jew? That I was naked, *"balls and all,"* hanging on the cross?" He said, "Charlie, not only did I become your sin and remove it from your life, I also took away your shame." The Lord showed me that in His culture, the worst form of shame and public humiliation was to show your nakedness. The crucifixion was designed to give the worst pain and public shame humanly possible. He reminded me that He didn't have a loincloth over himself like some would think. So not only did the cross forgive us of our sin, it also removed our shame and public humiliation—giving us an ability to walk in righteousness without shame.

So for years when I spoke about my past, there was very little regret or shame. But when Satan would try and dig up my history and use shame or humiliation trying to make me shrink back from being who God called me to be, I would ask the Lord how much He loved me. And so many times He would whisper, "Son, I love you *balls and all.*" The Lord would always remind me, "Charlie, you may still have the same social security number, but you are not that man anymore.

During my study time I was praying and trying to figure out how to preach about this part of the encounter I had always held so close. This was some of the secret-place relationship stuff that I had kept a secret from others for many years.

The Saturday before I was going to preach about this portion of my experience, I was having coffee on Saturday afternoon with Dianna Jones. She and her husband had moved to Florida from Nebraska and had been attending Identity Church for a little over a year. As we were sharing, the Lord opened my spiritual eyes and I saw that there was an issue blocking some deeper healing in her life. I saw it as a blockage, but the Lord would not give me any further details. Dianna and I had developed a close relationship very fast. Week after week she would sit in church and just cry and worship the Lord.

On Sunday, the Lord gave me a message about the removal of shame and I shared the story about the completion of what happened on the cross. My wife, Susie, was not very pleased with me because I spoke about Jesus being naked on the cross in my raw language that she has been trying to get me to curb a little. But this time the language needed to be there! This is Dianna's testimony how God was taking her from shame to innocence.

Dianna Jones Testimony

How could he possibly know? I thought. It was December 19, 2018, and I was sitting at my dining room table putting the last-minute touches on the baby blankets I had sewn for my great-grandsons. I was deep in thought, wondering what my family would be doing for the holidays. Truthfully, I was feeling a little melancholy; this was going to be our first Christmas in Florida since they were born. I was reminiscing of past years when my cell phone rang. To my delight, it was my oldest son, Rusty. He started out with the usual platitudes and then he said, "Mom, I need to ask you something." After a lingering pause, he stammered over his words, "Mom, in February 1969, did you give birth to a son?" There was a long silence and I remember trying to catch my breath. My first thought was, *Maybe I didn't hear him correctly*. Afraid to ask him to repeat the question, nothing came out of my mouth. At first, I wanted to deny it, but I just sat there, speechless.

No one in my family who was still alive knew about the son I gave up for adoption; no one except for an aunt who had driven me to the hospital knew about this, and she suffers from Alzheimer's. *What am I going to tell him?* I thought. *No one was supposed to know.* For fifty years, it was never spoken about, and I kept thinking that nobody would find out. How did this happen?

My son asked over the phone, "Mom, are you alright?"

"Yes, Rusty," I said.

"Mom I don't think badly of you. We've all made mistakes. I've made my share, and I'm not here to judge you." Then he added, "I want you to know that I've spoken with him. His name is Scott."

Ironically, Scott had been adopted by a family in the same city where three of my four children spent most of their junior and senior high school years. It was also the city where we became foster parents and adopted our fourth child and the city where I met my husband that same year. I later found out that his mother and I probably worked at the same place. It seems Rusty and Scott knew a lot of the same people. They shared a lot of the same interests and, strangely enough, they both shared the same profession: they both own their own painting companies.

Rusty was so excited about having another brother that he made plans to meet Scott and his wife, Lynn, in a few weeks. I wasn't quite certain at that point what to think; I only remember a deep sense of numbness overwhelmed me. I can't explain it. I was glad that they would meet, but was still speechless. I had been so careful not to let anyone know—not my friends or family; no one suspected anything.

When I was twenty-one, I had been working in Kansas City and just starting to grow up. I had disappointed my parents in the past, and I was trying to prove that I could make it on my own. Then I met John. Single and stupid, I made some really bad choices. Three months later I found myself pregnant, but my dreams of getting married and raising a family were quickly diminished when John became angry with me over something silly. He lashed out and struck me across the mouth, cutting my lip. Looking back now, I have a more lucid perspective, knowing his background. John had been a POW and probably suffered with PTSD, but at the time I didn't understand that, and didn't care; I just knew that I didn't deserve to be hit like that.

I left John right away. I knew I didn't want to be in an abusive relationship because I had seen what happened to women who allow that behavior, and one thing I knew was that I was not going to be with a man who would abuse me. I moved back home, got a job, and didn't tell anyone what happened—nor did they ask.

Every day I was afraid that someone would find out about my secret. I hid the guilt and shame by keeping everything buried. It's pretty crazy, but back in 1968, A-line dresses were popular, so I got away without anyone finding out—almost. I remember coming down the stairs at my parents' home, and my mother, who was entertaining a few relatives sitting at the dining room table, was just staring up at me. In that moment I knew that she knew. I was eight months along at that point.

The next day my mother asked me if I was pregnant. My world was collapsing. I could no longer deny my pregnancy, and the humiliation and shame was fresh and raw. I was mortified; I couldn't even take care of myself, so how could I raise a child? My mother knew what my dad would say (and probably do), so by the following week I had a little one-bedroom apartment in another city where my aunt and uncle lived. My mom and I never spoke about whether I was going to keep this child; it simply was understood that I was incapable of raising a child, and my family was not going to help me keep this baby.

Now my son was on the other end of the phone confronting me about this fifty-year secret. I gathered up the nerve to ask Rusty, "How did you find out?" Apparently, my niece had gone on one of the sites that check your ancestry and learned she had a first cousin, who also had gone on the same site to find out about his ancestry. She called Scott, and after putting together the dates, she knew he would more than likely be my son. She told Scott she was pretty certain she knew who his biological mother was and that he had four siblings. Later on, she called Rusty, and the rest is history.

At their first meeting, Rusty brought his wife and their youngest daughter, Lacey, to meet Scott and Lynn. The meeting was a great reunion, and Lacey called during their meeting to tell me how wonderful Scott is. While on the phone, Scott asked about his father. I had spent the last fifty years trying to bury the memory, and I honestly couldn't remember his last name. We spent three months together, but I don't remember. I told Scott he was a POW, and from looking at Scott's pictures, he looks a lot like his father. He said that he understood, but I'm certain he wasn't pleased that I couldn't remember his last name.

At the end of their weekend, Lacey called to report that her dad was so excited about having another brother, that he decided to call some of my aunts, cousins, and their families for a friendly "get-together" to introduce the newest member of the family. I was mortified—not of

Scott; I knew he was (and is) a gift from God, but because my secret sin was more than exposed—it was now broadcasted for the whole world! I have well over a hundred people in my family, and I was pretty confident that by now they all had heard the news.

Humiliated, embarrassed, and ashamed, I just sat there reflecting on the stigma of being an unwed mother all over—but even worse now, I was uncovered and exposed for the world to see. There were no badges of honor in the 60s. It was shameful, and I felt the pain and disgrace of it. What would everyone think? My husband and I are pastors! We had a ministry in Nebraska, and I also ministered in a nursing home just before a fire took our home and we moved to Florida. What kind of pastor was I? I was a disgrace to God!

Be Careful What You Pray

What was I going to do now? Sitting there in my puddle of shame, I felt the Lord's presence. He tenderly held me in His arms, comforting me. Then He reminded me about what I had asked Him a month or so earlier: "Lord, if there is any sin in me that's keeping me from getting closer to you, I give you permission to expose me, empty me, and give me clean hands and a pure heart so I can know You better." I had always preached that "the truth would set you free," but what I was feeling was anything but freedom!

Sunday morning, we sat in church. At Identity, I always enjoy Pastor Charlie's messages, but today I was feeling the weight of being downcast.

> Why are you cast down, O my soul, and why are you in turmoil within me? Hope in God; for I shall again praise him, my salvation and my God (Psalm 42:11).

The greatest thing that comes from faith in Christ is putting your hope in Him; it will not be in vain. If we put our trust in Jesus, all things will work together for those who love Him. I don't have to know how or why. Knowing that He loves me should be enough, but that particular Sunday, I was feeling Jesus's pain as Pastor Charlie described my Lord on the cross. I pictured Him hanging with blood running down His body onto the ground. He looked deformed as the nails were ripping His flesh, His face swollen, bruised and marred, and blood covered His entire body, making it impossible to even recognize my Lord. He was shamed, humiliated, disgraced and exposed, He was downcast. As I sat there, tears ran down my cheeks, seeing this picture of Jesus, and fully understanding that my sins and shame had nailed Him there, but, unlike me, He was innocent.

I listened to Pastor Charlie, mesmerized by the words coming out of his mouth; he was speaking directly to me. I wondered, *Did he somehow read my mind? Did God show him my sin yesterday when we had coffee? Had God revealed my secret to him? How did he know my disgrace?* Tears kept running down my face, then all at once he said something that resonated deep inside my soul. He said, "When Jesus hung on the cross, he was naked, *balls and all*, completely exposed." When I heard that, it was like an arrow shot straight from the cross and pierced through my heart. I held my breath. I felt the years of shame, guilt, disgrace, embarrassment, humiliation, and pain pouring out from my body like a river. Then he proclaimed that Jesus declared me shameless, cleared of my past sins and failures; they were all wiped away at Calvary.

When Jesus died for our salvation, He also declared us free from the shame of our past. Gone! A list of sins and failures just disappeared—there's nothing recorded in my book! Jesus declared me innocent. I don't understand it, but I knew my disgrace was erased.

> For He made Him who knew no sin *to be* sin for us, that we might become the righteousness of God in Him [to be innocent] (2 Cor. 5:21 NKJV).

Somehow Jesus had turned my morning into dancing; I was free at last, and for the first time in fifty years, my soul was at peace.

Pastor Charlie is a wonderful man, and he gets so much revelation and wisdom from the Lord that sometimes it can seem scary. Later that afternoon when I called him, he said, "What's up? I knew this morning's message really got to you." I just spilled my story out, unashamed. I told him about my pregnancy, how I had given my son up for adoption—everything I had gone through. I told him how that morning when he described Jesus on the cross naked and exposed, *balls and all*. My shame and humiliation from the last fifty years was released. Apparently he didn't get the same reaction from Susie; she felt he shouldn't have said it that way. But I told Pastor Charlie that those few words were what brought breakthrough and deliverance to me.

The same day my shame was removed, I got up the nerve to call Scott, and we talked for over three hours. He is a lovely man. He said that he has had a good life and was not angry about his past, only curious. He wasn't expecting anything from anyone and was only glad to know his extended family. We agreed to keep in touch, and over the next few months we would talk back and forth. God removed the shame so we could start a relationship without that blockage. God is a redeemer!

Complete Healing

The following weeks brought even more freedom. I didn't care who knew about my past, nor was I ashamed to announce that the Lord had blessed me with a beautiful son fifty years ago. One more piece was healed.

The following Sunday morning, Pastor Charlie asked if I was ready to give my testimony. I stood in front of my church, which included everyone listening to the Identity Internet podcast, and talked about my secret sin to the world. I told them about my past unashamedly! I was free from guilt and shame!

I felt like that part of my past was finally behind me. Then one week Pastor Charlie decided to preach about innocence. He had gone up north to Pennsylvania and preached a sermon about the "Baptism of Innocence." He began describing the brutality of the cross, and declared us innocent of our past, and then he called us forward to anoint us with oil and a kiss of innocence. As I stood in line, he moved in front of me and just paused. He looked a little perplexed, and then put oil on his hands and leaned forward, whispering in my ear, "Dianna, did anyone ever strike you across the mouth?" It took me off guard and tears began to flow freely. I looked at him and told him that the only man who had ever backhanded me was John. He told me that God instructed Him to turn his hand around and anoint me with the back of his hand because the Lord was going to completely heal that wound in my heart. I have been completely healed from the past!

> And I am sure of this, that he who began a good work in you will bring it to completion at the day of Jesus Christ (Phil. 1:6).

Conclusion

God's timing is so perfect. Dianna's testimony is proof that I heard correctly when God told me to use those "secret words" that had been so personal and private. God is good!

So let's debrief a little: Jesus became our sin, and then He removed public humiliation and personal shame during His crucifixion. We find the innocence portion of the crucifixion in some of Christ's final words to the Father.

> And when they came to the place that is called The Skull, there they crucified him, and the criminals, one on his right and one on his left. And Jesus said, "Father, forgive them, for they know not what they do." And they cast lots to divide his garments. And the people stood by, watching, but the rulers scoffed at him, saying, "He saved others; let him save himself, if he is the Christ of God, his Chosen One!" The soldiers also mocked him, coming up and offering him sour wine and saying, "If you are the King of the Jews, save yourself!" There was also an inscription over him, "This is the King of the Jews" (Luke 23:33–38).

When you look closely at these scriptures, you will find all the parts of the finished work of the cross. He was hung between two criminals. One mocked Jesus, and the other recognized his own guilt by the

THE BAPTISM OF INNOCENCE

innocence he saw in Jesus, and the guilty man asked for mercy. As the brutal death came to an end, the soldiers were gambling over Jesus's clothing that had been stripped to expose His nakedness. Then Jesus was talking to the Father who had executed this plan before the foundation of the world to remove the sin of every person ever born.

Remember, Jesus took on the sin of the world, not just your sin. Looking around, He asks the Father to forgive them. Jesus is telling the Father they are innocent. Who? The two thieves? The soldiers that pierced His side? The gamblers on the ground? The mocking rulers?

I've come to the conclusion that the finished work of the cross includes taking the sins of the world on Himself and the forgiveness of sin. It includes the public humiliation and shame He suffered, and with His final breath He declared us all innocent. You see, Jesus was the only one who could redeem and restore us back to innocence, because He was without sin and innocent.

When I had my encounter with the baptism of innocence, I had to embrace it for myself and let it do a deep work in my heart. I had three days of walking in a fresh relationship with Holy Spirit and reliving the childlike innocence. During those three days, I had to deal with every broken relationship that I needed forgiveness for. I also had to deal with paperwork I held on myself, or—even worse—that Satan held against me. Those three days fit the pattern of death, burial, and resurrection.

You must deal with yourself first before you deal with others. You can't give away something you don't have or haven't experienced yourself. Dealing with your own records of wrong is sometimes the hardest thing to do!

After declaring Randy innocent, I experienced a fresh relationship with God that was based on my own innocence—and I did not want to give up this new love walk. So when God pushed me to do it by faith, I trusted Him with a renewed childlikeness to help me walk out the process. In a vision, I saw all of the paperwork I had kept within myself of the past records of wrong that I held against Randy. If I had not dealt with my own records first, I would have never dealt with Randy's. My motivation was the value I placed on my renewed innocent love walk with Holy Spirit. Love holds no record of wrong!

When I value His presence more than my pain, I can walk in peace and power, knowing I am innocent.

God is love and in 1 Corinthians 13, we find a wonderful description of love:

> Love is patient, love is kind. It does not envy, it does not boast, it is not proud. It is not rude, it is not self-seeking, it is not easily angered, it keeps no record of wrongs. Love does not delight in evil but rejoices with the truth. It always protects, always trusts, always hopes, always perseveres (1 Cor. 13:4–7 NIV).

***

Wisdom Keys:

1. Jesus was naked to remove your shame and public humiliation.
2. You can't give away something you don't have or haven't experienced.
3. When you value His presence more than your pain, then you will walk in peace and power.

Chapter 6: No Paperwork!

Papa Jack Taylor was having a sons and daughters gathering in Titusville, Florida, which is about an hour away from my house. Papa Jack was pretty emphatic about me showing up for a few days. With as many sons gatherings that I have been to, I knew Papa Jack was feeling that either there was a specific reason for me to be there to minister or he just needed me there for him personally. So when Jack asked for the third time, I knew he needed me there. It has always worked out where the Lord uses us as "brother teams" in those settings. I knew that Bill Vanderbush was going to be there in the evening. There's something supernatural that happens when brothers get together under a spiritual father's authority who turns us loose to be who God made us to be. This father-son paradigm in the family of God is, in my opinion, the kingdom system of government that will bring heaven to earth.

I had extended a ministry trip that weekend, and was honestly looking for a reason not to go. But I could not get out of my prior engagement, and I still felt the Spirit on the inside urging me to go and spend a few days with Papa Jack. As I prayed, the Lord spoke to me and said, "I have given you the dream job that allows you to work on the road, and you have a team in place to be able to do both work and ministry." Then the Lord told me that I was needed, and to "be myself." (Many times, being myself doesn't work out to my advantage.) So with the Lord's approval it was a done deal, and I had to go. I had a heart of anticipation and expectation that the Lord was going to do something special.

I had just gotten a new motorcycle and was inspired to take it on a mini road trip. At 2:30 in the afternoon I showed up to the retreat center in Titusville. I pulled up with my new decked-out motorcycle, with loud pipes and loud music blaring. I began unloading the motorcycle and looked in the foyer of the retreat center, expecting that Jack was having a teaching session or group sharing. There could have been forty men and women, but there were only two couples just getting to know each other.

As I walked in, I heard the Lord reveal to me a few things about the two couples that were present. After talking to them, I found out that they were both in ministry and were very well-seasoned people of God. One couple had moved from Australia. The lady from Australia made my "baby jump" on the inside of my spirit, and put my spirit man on full alert—it was going to be a fun afternoon. But as I looked at them in the spirit, I was a little intimidated at first with how much authority they both carried. Both couples were generals in the kingdom. The lady from Australia was trying to discern me at first, and I started to shut down to become a student, listen, and learn something.

The other couple, Tim and Janet, were also very seasoned ministers of the gospel. As I tried to read the room, I was leaning toward my default assumption that leaders in a church of this caliber oftentimes have a religious spirit. Many times, when I feel the Lord push me out front, I begin with my rough testimony to see if they can get past the rawness and discern the anointing to find out that God wants to do something supernatural. That has been part of my healing from the abuse of the leadership I was raised under. If I'm not careful, I can destroy relationships out of fear of being rejected (but I will save that lesson for a different book).

It wasn't long after I finished writing the book *From Rape to Righteousness: Redeeming the Bride of Christ*, so it was fresh in my heart. That testimony would have made the religious spirit manifest, and I would have taken a different form of ministry. But there was a maturity in the room with these people, and it opened the door for me to start heading in the direction the Lord was showing me: the story of the baptism of innocence.

NO PAPERWORK!

I started telling them how I had this encounter with the Lord and had received the baptism of innocence, how God baptized me again with a childlike feeling of innocence that I had not had in over twenty-five years. I told about the encounter with Randy in the New York conference and how our broken relationship was restored. I shared that during that conference, as I started to defend my stance to the Lord against Randy, I saw my paperwork of all the wrongs that I felt he had committed against me and against others—and I was even offended for God. I had several sheets of paperwork in my head, that was my defense, and I tried to use them as an excuse not to obey the Lord. But He gave me only one option: declare him innocent. The Lord spoke very loudly to me: "LOSE YOUR PAPERWORK AND DECLARE HIM INNOCENT." Lose your paperwork? The verse about love came to my mind again.

> Love is patient, Love is kind. It does not envy, it does not boast, it is not proud. It does not dishonor others, it is not self-seeking, it is not easily angered, **it keeps not record of wrongs**. Love does not delight in evil but rejoices with the truth. It always protects, always trusts, always hopes, always preserves. Love never fails (1 Corinthians 13:4–8 NIV, emphasis mine).

The true miracle was that Randy had to supernaturally lose his paperwork to be able to receive the baptism of innocence. Randy and I have called this one of the mysteries of the kingdom—a verbal declaration and a supernatural impartation that burns up the paperwork and destroys all the records of wrongs that we keep in our heads and hearts. Many times, it's the paperwork that the enemy uses to torment us.

As I retold this story to the two couples, "lose your paperwork" was highlighted in my delivery, specifically to Tim and Janet. It was so real when the Lord showed me papers with all the record of wrongs that had been done to me through this covenant breaking issue. As I processed the paperwork details, Tim asked me to be more specific. He asked, "What does paperwork mean?"

THE BAPTISM OF INNOCENCE

I told him that it's like when there is a divorce between two parties. There is paperwork justifying the separation of relationship, influence, property, friendship, etc. Many times in a divorce, the wife will even go back to her maiden name so as to not have a day-to-day reference of her ex-husband. That's paperwork; in the kingdom, you get mercy in the same proportion that you give it.

Let's take a look at the parable of the unmerciful servant in Matthew chapter 18.

> Then Peter came up and said to him, "Lord, how often will my brother sin against me, and I forgive him? As many as seven times?" Jesus said to him, "I do not say to you seven times, but seventy-seven times. Therefore the kingdom of heaven may be compared to a king who wished to settle accounts with his servants. When he began to settle, one was brought to him who owed him ten thousand talents. And since he could not pay, his master ordered him to be sold, with his wife and children and all that he had, and payment to be made. So the servant fell on his knees, imploring him, 'Have patience with me, and I will pay you everything.' And out of pity for him, the master of that servant released him and forgave him the debt. But when that same servant went out, he found one of his fellow servants who owed him a hundred denarii, and seizing him, he began to choke him, saying, 'Pay what you owe.' So his fellow servant fell down and pleaded with him, 'Have patience with me, and I will pay you.' He refused and went and put him in prison until he should pay the debt. When his fellow servants saw what had taken place, they were greatly distressed, and they went and reported to their master all that had taken place. Then his master summoned him and said to him, 'You wicked servant! I forgave you all that debt because you pleaded with me. And should not you have had mercy on your fellow servant, as I had mercy on you?' And in anger his master delivered him to the jailers, until he should pay

all his debt. So also my heavenly Father will do to every one of you, if you do not forgive your brother from your heart" (Matthew 18:21–35).

Peter started off by asking, "What is the requirement of forgiveness, so I can be good in God's eyes—seven times?" I have had some of the same thoughts when it came to my issues of unforgiveness and bitterness: *Lord, help me meet Your requirement so I can get on with my agenda.* But if you look at all that the Lord has forgiven me from, I should be full of mercy and grace. The only way to prove you have something in the kingdom is to give it away. There are many teachings about the principles of sowing and reaping. It also works with love, innocence, mercy, and grace. You get what you give away.

> For judgment is without mercy to one who has shown no mercy. Mercy triumphs over judgment (James 2:13).

As the conversation with both couples was coming to an end, I started asking the Lord how He wanted me to handle this. Up until this time, I had laid hands on people, kissed them on the cheek, and decreed over them to receive the baptism of innocence. I have seen that the overwhelming power of God cleans and renews many people as I do that. The Lord spoke to me that this was a very special couple, and I was to do it differently. He showed me that their journey had been a long and very hard season of pain, betrayal, and great loss that had been horrific to endure, and He didn't want a person in the middle of what He was doing. I had this sense it was a do-or-die moment for them, just like it was for me when God told me that I needed to obey or it could be the last message I would ever preach.

I asked the Lord what He wanted me to do. He told me to go get a wet washcloth and a dry towel, and I was to wash their feet and pray over them, declaring that the pain and dust from the last season was finished and cleaned up. I told them that I had always given a kiss on the cheek and declared the person to receive the baptism on innocence, but God told me to wash their feet and that He would visit them and kiss them Himself. I even said they would receive the baptism of innocence that

THE BAPTISM OF INNOCENCE

night from God. I have found that receiving the baptism of innocence is just the beginning; proving you got it is where the rubber meets the road. To prove you have something in the kingdom requires your ability to give it away.

That night when Jack opened ministry time with the whole group, there was such a loving spirit in the room. Papa Jack introduced Bill Vanderbush and me to the group that had already been together for a few days. Like I said, there is something supernatural when a spiritual father is overseeing a meeting from a kingdom prospective with hungry sons and daughters. Bill is always "Mr. Revelator," and we started the meeting talking about grace and then on to baptism of innocence.

Bill has written a book called *Reckless Grace*, and we have had conversations about how the baptism of innocence gives proper boundaries to grace that will mature us into Christlikeness.

The next morning, Tim and Janet gave their testimony on receiving the baptism of innocence the night before, and then Tim started talking about some computer files he had on his laptop where he had detailed files of wrongs and betrayals that had been committed against Him and Janet with some people who had been in ministry with them and had stolen their possessions. Tim's files were detailed enough to hand over to an attorney, some going back twenty years. Tim and Janet had a major choice to make, and they could feel the conviction from the Holy Spirit. How can we prove we have received the baptism of innocence and not give it away to others who have wronged us? I have said it before, but it is worth repeating again: receiving is the easy part. Giving it away to others requires you to burn the paperwork!

That morning, Papa Jack started laying hands for impartation on some of his sons and daughters, releasing a blessing to us. What we didn't know at the time was that some of Tim's leadership had given him a word that on this trip to Florida, Jack was going to release a "mantle of advancement insight" over them and their ministry. So it was with great expectation that they were receiving a blessing from Papa Jack. After the morning service, we all blessed each other and went our separate ways.

NO PAPERWORK!

Tim and Janet went to Orlando for the night. While they were there, they realized that the same day Jack prayed over them fell on the twenty-year anniversary of when they started their church. As they walked through the healing and the blessing that the Lord had done, they put their hands together as they went through and deleted all the files on the computer of people who had wronged them. Delete, delete, delete, delete. That is what we are calling burning up the paperwork! Afterward, they took communion together to complete the removal of any residue from old paperwork that may not have been covered in their minds—the blood covers all.

Later on, Tim preached that this act of burning the paperwork opened a door that God had promised them twenty-two years ago through a prophecy from Cindy Jacobs, two years before they started their church. Tim went into great detail about the word that had been prayed over them, which they believed they were now walking in. He said that the last part of her word stated that their ministry would not be paperwork, but covenant. Tim had always thought it referred to denominational paperwork versus kingdom covenant relationships. It doesn't take long being around Tim to figure out he is all about relationship in the kingdom.

When God highlighted the last part of that prophecy to Tim, he was shocked. This was a twenty-two-year-old prophecy. It was like God saving the best wine till last, when most of the people leave the wedding feast (see John chapter 2).

Tim said he had a blind spot in his life so that he couldn't see it, and as they received the baptism of innocence, they also had the humility to delete the paperwork and give it away. Tim expressed that it was what had been holding them back from the promises that the Lord had given them many years ago.

The Enemy's Paperwork against Us

Years ago, I learned about paperwork from a different angle when I was dealing with the enemy over an issue I had. I went into the courts of heaven, and the enemy had a case against me. He had a stack of

THE BAPTISM OF INNOCENCE

paperwork filled with accusations, and he was telling the heavenly court that I was not worthy of the blessing of the Lord because of all the paperwork he had. Let's take a look at Scripture to reflect on this.

> Then he showed me Joshua the high priest standing before the angel of the Lord, and Satan standing at his right hand to accuse him. And the Lord said to Satan, "The Lord rebuke you, O Satan! The Lord who has chosen Jerusalem rebuke you! Is not this a brand plucked from the fire?" Now Joshua was standing before the angel, clothed with filthy garments. And the angel said to those who were standing before him, "Remove the filthy garments from him." And to him he said, "Behold, I have taken your iniquity away from you, and I will clothe you with pure vestments." And I said, "Let them put a clean turban on his head." So they put a clean turban on his head and clothed him with garments. And the angel of the Lord was standing by. And the angel of the Lord solemnly assured Joshua, "Thus says the Lord of hosts: If you will walk in my ways and keep my charge, then you shall rule my house and have charge of my courts, and I will give you the right of access among those who are standing here" (Zech. 3:1–7).

Satan is an accuser and a legalist, and he uses the legal system against us. When we hold onto our paperwork against a brother or someone who wronged us, the enemy will bring a case with paperwork against *us* into the heavenly realm and do everything in his power to withhold what is rightfully ours. If you look at this passage, there are some very important keys.

1. Satan is an accuser and a legalist.
2. Satan always wins when we don't show up.
3. Satan wins when we have filthy garments. You get filthy garments when you hold paperwork on others.
4. When we get a new, clean turban on our heads, we get the mind of Christ, and our thinking changes into His thinking.

NO PAPERWORK!

5. We get authority when we walk in God's ways and keep the principles and purposes of the kingdom.
6. We will have rulership in God's house, charge of the courts of heaven, and heavenly access through "Jacob's Ladder."

Satan's real goal is to drag you from the throne room back into the courtroom where you have to defend yourself.

This takes me back to John 20:22–23:

> And with that he breathed on them and said, Receive the Holy Spirit. If you forgive anyone his sins, they are forgiven: if you do not forgive them, they are not forgiven (NIV).

That is ruling in the house of God and taking charge of His courts!

Removing paperwork is very hard to do when you have a distorted view of God as a good Father. When I had to deal with all my paperwork against Randy, I was telling the Father that I wanted to hold onto my right to reject him with legal proof. But the Father was asking me to trust Him. The baptism of innocence produces a renewed childlikeness—and pure, innocent childlikeness has its foundation in trusting of the Father. It's about trusting Him for protection and maturing from childishness to Christlikeness. Don't confuse childlikeness with childishness. They are not even close.

One time, one of my spiritual sons, Anthony, was having weight loss surgery, and he asked me and our friend Eva to pray over him before he went for surgery. Eva and I had discipled Anthony for years, and he considered us to be spiritual parents to him. We used to talk about spiritual things for hours, and her family had been very instrumental in my spiritual life and my ability to have a church. I wouldn't be anywhere near my current situation without their support and love for me.

The problem was that Eva and I had a disagreement over some doctrine, and we had been out of fellowship for eight years. So when Anthony told me that Eva was going to meet us Monday night after our men's group to pray for him, I was a little concerned. We had been around each other very little, only for funerals and public events—but the heart-to-heart relationship of trust had been broken for years.

That morning in prayer I told the Lord that it was like we were divorced parents, who loved the child enough to come into the same room and bless the son we both have cared for over twenty years. The Lord asked me, "Why don't you burn the divorce papers between you two, and let the baptism of innocence heal both of your hearts?" That convicted me, and I declared myself innocent from all that I had done to hurt Eva—even the things that I believed I was still right in doing, but was used to wound and make a righteous stand in the wrong way.

As I released the paperwork against Eva, I felt all the years of love come back, the reality of the hundreds of hours we spent walking together and discussing the Word of God. I was reminded that after my mother passed away, I had asked Eva to be a spiritual mother to me. My heart was cleaned, and with no paperwork, I could see her in the proper view. I truly would not be in the position I am without this relationship. It's amazing when baptism of innocence removes the paperwork how a godly view returns and gratefulness comes over you.

After the men's meeting, Eva came to the church—the very building that her family's generosity had made possible to use as a church for the last twelve years. Eva and I went into my office to pray over Anthony, and when we finished, we sat down and started talking. We talked about how she and her husband, Joe, are building houses again, and we caught up from lost time together.

As we talked, I started to unpack the baptism of innocence, and Eva caught it by the Spirit. It was like old times with God giving us revelation. Eva looked at me and said, "What do I do? I have paperwork on you. I have a list of records of wrong about you."

I walked up to her, kissed her on the cheek, and Eva received the baptism of innocence. It was the most incredible Holy Spirit moment I had seen in a long time. Eva began to explain how a customer was taking advantage of them and costing them a lot of money in the construction of a new home. She said that he manipulated paperwork against Joe, and it was eating her up on the inside.

Then she asked how to deal with the paperwork that makes you want to get revenge. I explained that the baptism of innocence brings back childlikeness and gives us faith that the Father will protect us. When we trust in Him to protect us, He will give us wisdom and take away the need to get revenge.

Avenge vs. Revenge

Avenge is a verb. To avenge something is to punish a wrongdoing with the intent of seeing justice done. God the Father built His throne on justice and righteousness.

> Righteousness and justice are the foundation of your throne;
> steadfast love and faithfulness go before you (Psalm 89:14).

Revenge can be used either as a noun or a verb. It is more personal and is less concerned with justice, and more about retaliation through inflicting harm.

Avenge and *revenge* both imply inflicting pain or harming in return for pain or harm inflicted on us, people, or causes to which we are loyal. The two words used to be interchangeable, but have been differentiated because now convey widely diverse ideas. *Avenge* is now restricted to inflicting punishment as an act of retributive justice or as vindication of propriety: for instance, to avenge a murder by bringing a criminal to trial. *Revenge* implies inflicting pain or harm to retaliate for real or fancied wrongs.

God never intends for us to be pushovers and let people take advantage of us; He wants us to be able to trust that when we are in relationships, offenses will come. It's how we handle them that matters. Many times, I have to wait on the Lord to see what is pleasing to Him and make sure that a spirit of revenge doesn't become my fuel to be right, and therefore not righteous.

THE BAPTISM OF INNOCENCE

Forgiveness is the act of releasing the desire to punish or get revenge on someone for an offense. It's an act of grace, so you cannot force it or pretend it's done. You have to recognize the offense and feel the pain before the release becomes real. Then the baptism of innocence gives you the ability to move from forgiveness to removing paperwork and declaring others innocent.

When we have paperwork about what others did to us, it's like we have put them in a time capsule and think that God has only changed us. But when we burn up the paperwork, God can reveal to us that others have also grown in grace and love. I believe this is one of the foundations of the ministry of reconciliation that is needed for the body of Christ to be able to walk together.

A Vision as Joseph

I am convinced that in my life, the revelation of the baptism of innocence started a few years ago when I was asking the Father why I hadn't seen some of the promises He had given to me. I went into a vision, and He showed me standing on a national stage in the land of Egypt. You know the story of Joseph in Genesis chapters 37-50. He had a dream that his whole family bowed down to him. Then his brothers sold him into slavery, but the Lord was with Joseph, even in the midst of a horrible situation. Eventually, he was exalted to a place of being able to rescue God's people. It is important to note that the dreams and promises of God will test you.

> When he summoned a famine on the land and broke all supply of bread, he had sent a man ahead of them, Joseph, who was sold as a slave. His feet were hurt with fetters; his neck was put in a collar of iron; until what he had said came to pass, the word of the LORD tested him (Psalm 105:16–19).

Look at how *The Passion Translation* puts that last verse:

> God's promise to Joseph purged his character until it was time for his dreams to come true.

So in this vision, I was on a stage, and Pharaoh was introducing me—not Joseph—to the whole nation of Egypt. Pharaoh had put his kingly robes on me with gold chains around my neck. He then put the signet ring on my finger to be able to do business and rule on his behalf. Then Pharaoh told all of his governmental leaders and the whole nation of Egypt that there was no one with more authority in the whole nation, other than himself, than me!

As I looked over the crowd, I found Potiphar's wife. When we locked eyes, I saw fear in her heart. She knew what she had done to me, and I saw fear grip her heart that I might retaliate. (I kind of liked it when I saw her squirming in her seat.) I looked into her eyes and mouthed the words, "You can keep my coat." She started crying and put her head down.

As I came out of this vision, the Lord said that there were still some things on the inside of me that needed to be healed before the promises could be released. I argued with the Lord. I said, "You know that I have passed that test before and used the sword on myself and not others. I wouldn't have hurt Potiphar's wife, even though her false accusation was responsible for pain, rejection, and additional prison time."

The Lord said, "Yes, I know that, and you have proven that to be a strength; but I am after your motivations, not just your actions." He said that for a season He was going to work out of me the wrong fuel I used to feed my passions and showed me that some of my motivations had been fueled to prove that my critics were wrong. He allowed the wrong fuel for a season, but would not be able to trust me with the authority He promised if that is what was fueling my passions. He also showed me that my false belief that *"He was not good all the time"* was the root of my insecurity, and when I burn insecurity as my fuel, it comes off as pride and arrogance. This turned into a revelation that when the fuel of innocence is burned for motivation, it is witnessed by others as true humility.

I have been walking out this baptism of innocence encounter for over a year now. A few weeks ago, I had to do some pastoring Sunday morning with one of my leaders, and missed half of worship. As I walked into worship, the presence of the Lord hit me and He said, "Charlie, I can trust you with Potiphar's wife!" I fell down at the altar and worshiped; I became so grateful that the Lord had removed the fuel of my motivation that displeased Him and had replaced it with the fuel of innocence. I felt like true humility finally showed up. When true humility is present, it makes you grateful to the Lord because only He can do that.

Removing the paperwork was preparation for the Lord to remove the wrong fuel in my life and replace it with innocence. When innocence is the fuel we burn, purity and holiness with power as the outcome.

***

Wisdom Keys:

1. Lose the paperwork you hold against yourself first; only then can you burn up what you are holding against others.
2. The baptism of innocence is one of the mysteries of the kingdom.
3. The only way to prove you have something in the kingdom is to give it away.
4. Receiving is the easier part, giving it away requires true sacrifice.
5. Satan wins when you have filthy garments resulting from holding paperwork on others.
6. Satan's real goal is to drag you from the throne room back into the courtroom to defend yourself.
7. The baptism of innocence returns your ability to have gratefulness as a filter over your eyes.
8. You have to recognize the offense and feel the pain before release becomes real.
9. When innocence is the fuel we burn, purity and holiness with power is the outcome.

Chapter 7: The Boundaries of Grace

This chapter has been a long time coming for me personally. When the Lord speaks to me, it normally gets me in hot water. I have to admit it has made the journey interesting, to say the least!

At one time, God was trying to introduce me to the grace message. He kept telling me to order a certain book that I saw on a Christian website. The book was titled *Miracle Workers, Reformers, and the New Mystics* by John Crowder. The problem was that I had at least fifteen books on my nightstand that I had not read yet, and Susie had me on lockdown—no new book purchasing until I finished reading the books I already had.

So for weeks the Lord would tell me that this book would change my life and ministry, but I had to have Susie's permission to make purchases outside of our budget. You see, there was a time when I was told and believed that you can't out-give God. That's a bunch of religious garbage, and the Lord had me submit to my wife in that area of our finances. But every week or so, the Lord would tell me to buy that book. When I looked at it online, there was a short synopsis on the website:

> Two thousand years of miracle workers and seers crammed into one generation. The fiery bowls of heaven are being poured out through an extreme body of spiritual forerunners. Are you called to walk among them?

THE BAPTISM OF INNOCENCE

Miracle Workers, Reformers, and the New Mystics contains more than seventy photos, illustrations, and biographies of men and women whose lives have demonstrated the phenomenal throughout the ages. Let their stories inspire you to join their ranks as part of this coming revival generation.

This review kept burning in my heart as the Lord was telling me to purchase this book. I told God that He had put me under Susie's authority when it came to spending money, and if He wanted me to read it, He had to tell someone to give me a copy of this book. I wasn't going to disobey my wife. About two weeks later, a member of my church walked up to me and said that he purchased a book at a garage sale for fifty cents and God told him to give it to me. Guess which book it was? Bingo! Yes, God was very serious about my need to read this book.

John Crowder Meetings

As I read this book about the mystics and reformers of history, my faith was ignited, and I was ready to be what God had called me to be: a "Reformer." Just as I was finishing the book, a friend from Orlando, George, called me and wanted to know what was going on in my life. I started to tell him about how God made sure that I got a copy of the book by John Crowder. After George let me rant and rave about what I was reading, he asked if I wanted to meet John Crowder. Of course I did! This book was changing my life. It was written like a history book about miracle workers and reformers with historical backgrounds, like a textbook of how God works through His people in modern times. John wrote like a highly-educated theologian, with great wisdom and maturity in a book that was fact-based.

We hung up, and about ten minutes later I got a phone call from John Crowder. I knew God was working in a supernatural way. As John and I spoke, we made plans to have a series of meetings at my church. This was God—and I didn't want to miss what God was up to. At the time, I was letting a local pastor with over 120 youth use my building to do church on our off nights, so I asked if he wanted to partner with me on these meetings. I was so excited to be a part of what God was up to.

As we started promoting the meeting, the pastor I asked to partner with me came and told me that he wanted no part of John Crowder or his ministry. Then he showed me some online videos where John was wild and crazy, doing things like toking the Holy Ghost like a joint and shooting up Jesus in the main vein, getting high on the "Most High." It tweaked my religious spirit, and made me wonder if I had heard God.

But all along there was this "knowing" in my spirit that it was God, and I didn't want to miss what God was doing, in spite of the cost. I put out flyers and did advertising to promote the meetings—crossing my fingers the whole time, wondering what in the world I had gotten myself into. The first night of a three-night meeting was interesting when a group of "John Crowder haters" flooded the parking lot with megaphones. They called John a false prophet and put out flyers on car windshields stating that John Crowder was a false prophet, telling everyone that we were going to hell for hosting these meeting.

As I write this chapter, I am reminded of the dog that bit me the night I preached about the baptism of innocence, and how the Lord told me not to overreact because it was a sign. Here were the same religious "dogs," biting and growling and trying to devour me with fear using their twisted truth with hate.

But there was something on the inside of me that gave me the courage to know that I was on the right track. Three days of John Crowder and the grace message on steroids was triggering every religious spirit in me and my whole church. But God was in the house! During those meetings, Susie got free from something that was holding her back. She got drunk in the Holy Ghost with my oldest grandson, and had a Holy Ghost encounter which did something on the inside of her. Just that made those meetings worth it. There were a lot of lost relationships, and it killed a lot of religion we had been part of. I know Susie had been touched by God when offering time came and she started writing a check that we had to scramble to cover. That is a sign of freedom.

John stayed in my home with his son, and we spent time together on my boat on the river relaxing and having fellowship. You get to know someone when you see them with family and overhear phone calls with their wife and other people. John was the first grace preacher that was out of the box, and I could not find a biblical problem with the message. What became an issue was that many of my young leaders got the grace message and misinterpreted it, dropping out of places of responsibility and leaving the structured church, calling it the gospel. They would not adhere to sound advice and some have never returned to church, or even part of a structured church family, and they are not in leadership any longer.

Aftermath of the Grace Message

Susie and I were really blessed when we went to Alabama to a meeting that John had. I was trying to figure out how to run a church and walk in this grace message at the same time. John is a stand-up preacher of the grace message, but it didn't have the boundaries needed for maturity within the structure I had at the time. I believed the grace message John preached; I reviewed his life and lifestyle, but could not put it into practice and maintain the church at the same time. In my opinion, he blew up my church and it took me two years to recover. But what do you do when you don't disagree with the message? You keep looking for the proper boundaries.

I asked God to help me with my dilemma. He told me that "Grace is an offensive empowerment to walk in holiness, not a defensive excuse to walk in sin."

I found that my relationship with John Crowder would come into play a few years later when a leader of many churches used some of our sound equipment for a religious detox cruise with John Crowder. It was just like it was spelled, out to detox from religion—and there is no one better at that then John Crowder. When my friend came to return the equipment, he looked like death warmed over. See, he had just been chastised by the leadership of his denomination, and was pretty beat up for promoting this detox cruise. With my experience and love for John Crowder, I was able to give firsthand advice and heal some wounds.

What do we do as leaders when the message lines up with Scripture and the true power of grace is rejected and called false? I felt the frustration and the dilemma the body of Christ is having with this grace, or as some would call it: sloppy grace. The reason we call it "sloppy grace" is because we can't control it. There, I said it—it's all about control.

As a leader, I love my people and feel responsible for them. And when they get the grace message, the places of their immature character will be exposed and will do damage to their moral life. I have seen divorce come into play, and they feel grace will permit it. But the Lord showed me that love out of balance is one of the worst kinds of control a leader can have. I love my people, so at first I labeled this as "sloppy grace" and rejected the message and the true power of grace.

Then I was exposed to a group of leaders with the grace message who believed that God had no issue with someone living a homosexual lifestyle, and even promoted them into leadership in the church! This was a game-changer for me, and I wrote off the sloppy grace message. I've lost some of my dogmas, but not my belief on these matters of Christian life in the kingdom—those have not changed.

Identity Is the Key

Years later I came into relationship with Bill Vanderbush, a "grace" preacher, and I was a little curious what his stand would be for how to deal with my issues of the "sloppy grace" message and proper order in the kingdom. After the first set of meetings, I told him about my dilemma and fallout with the grace message, not with John Crowder, but my inability to walk it out. To my surprise, he gave me a pretty good answer that I could live with—identity is the key!

That hit home for me. In 2008, we had started our church and named it "One Kingdom Fellowship." We had just changed the name to "Identity Church," and our slogan is "Where Sonship is Revealed." So I was very direct with Bill about my concerns, not wanting sloppy grace to become an excuse for a poor lifestyle. He explained that if a brother is weak in an area, we should get closer to him to show that his behavior is not lining up with his identity in Christ. Bill used grace to reveal our true identity in Christ. So if the behavior was incorrect, he didn't attack actions directly;

THE BAPTISM OF INNOCENCE

he looked to realign a person's identity. He said that when there is a false identity of whose we are, then we will have a false identity of who we are. When identity comes into alignment with Christ and the Father, behavior and lifestyle will follow.

I didn't let Bill off the hook easily; I even pushed him about how to deal with leaders who were pushing lifestyles that don't line up with Scripture. Bill told me that if you can't get a friend or a leader to line up with their true identity in Christ, sometimes you have to back off and start praying for an open door to love and demonstrate a Christlikeness that will bring change.

I believe in John Crowder and Bill Vanderbush's message of grace. In the opening part of Bill's and Brit Eaton's book *Reckless Grace,* Bill writes about the grace message:

> Grace is, in my opinion, the most powerful evangelistic tool the church of Jesus Christ has never used. Individually and corporately, we cling to our offenses in a fit of so-called "righteous anger," and we completely miss out on an opportunity to witness God's grace in action. It needs to change. Now.
>
> It's from a place of both great humility and strong authority that I share these truths with you as one who has both received and released the grace of God. The joy that comes with being a steward of God's relentless, radical, reckless grace is simply too good not to share, and so important, I'm willing to risk it all to do so.
>
> Building a case for grace in an offense-filled world isn't for the faint of heart. And yet, by the grace of God, here I go. Here we go, together.[1]

As I read this, I wanted to say that I was completely convinced about the power of the grace message. But here is where the baptism of innocence has helped me with my personal dilemma of how to walk in reckless grace and come to maturity in Christ.

---

1. Bill Vanderbush and Brit Eaton, *Reckless Grace*, (2018).

When I had my encounter with the baptism of innocence, there was a purity that came into my heart that religion had stolen from me for years. I had lost my childlike relationship with the Father and was living on the hamster wheel of performance.

When He baptized me with innocence, the Holy Spirit started teaching again to be childlike. When innocence replaces guilt, there is a teachability that brings us to maturity. Innocence takes the victim out of my voice. In innocence, the Father reveals places of false identity, immaturity, and bad behavior that needs to change. When I'm innocent, it is not punishment, but discipline. That will change my personal identity of who I am, and then behavior and lifestyle will follow.

> At that time the disciples came to Jesus, saying, "Who is the greatest in the kingdom of heaven?" And calling to him a child, he put him in the midst of them and said, "Truly, I say to you, unless you turn and become like children, you will never enter the kingdom of heaven. Whoever humbles himself like this child is the greatest in the kingdom of heaven (Matt. 18:1–4).

The disciples were debating over who was the greatest, and Jesus told them to "turn" and become like a child. That's the baptism of innocence. It gives the grace to turn, brings true humility, and shows us who we are in the kingdom. It changes our identity.

Two Triangles

I never asked to become a pastor of a congregation, much less operate a church building. In 2007 I was flying home from China with my father and some others who had just spent twenty days ministering, and the Lord wanted to talk to me. As I review this encounter from thirteen years ago, I have found that the grace message and the baptism of innocence have and will become the pressure that will bring the systems together so that the kingdom will be revealed in balance and bring generations to a godly lifestyle.

THE BAPTISM OF INNOCENCE

We had a great time in China and boarded the plane for a twenty-two-hour flight home. As I sat in my seat, revisiting the events of the trip with the Lord, He asked me how I saw the condition of the church in China. I'd always heard that the underground house churches of China had become the new role model of what God was doing on the earth. What I saw in the house churches there definitely has a place, and can be effective in expanding the kingdom. There is also a huge aboveground church in China, but the two are divided.

I saw two completely separate triangles, with the house church as one triangle and the aboveground church as the other, yet the two triangles never find the "holy sweet spot" in the middle where they blended. I saw the same divided systems in the church in America. As I pondered this, the Lord spoke to me and said, "I want to show you what I'm about to do on the earth."

I went into a vision and saw the two triangles under extreme pressure getting mashed together. As the two triangles came together, I saw that they formed the Star of David. Then in the middle of the Star of David I saw a picture of Christ. The Lord said, "Charlie, the body of Christ is leaving the church age, and I'm in the process of birthing the kingdom. The old system still has foundational principles from which I can bring my kingdom." Then He said that the older would serve the younger.

Pastoral

Apostolic

He told me that the church had entered into the same season as when John the Baptist started crying in the wilderness. He asked me, "Why haven't you asked Me why I had John the Baptist's head cut off?"

I asked the Lord if He actually did that. I thought Satan did it. He then informed me that He was sovereign.

He said, "I made sure that the old system of the law and the prophets was finished so I would be the head of the church." With the beheading of John the Baptist and the finished work of the cross, Jesus is the one who became our sin; He released grace and the baptism of innocence to all of us. Jesus is the giver of grace and innocence.

I have been pastoring for over twelve years now and I can look back at the issues I've had with a religious spirit (that some would say is borderline legalism) and sloppy grace with no structure. I have had to balance my beliefs as I worked through the seasons with the Lord. After the baptism of innocence came a balancing within my leadership style. When the core beliefs change in a person, so will his behaviors. Sometimes it takes a while for the change to be lasting because we still have to hunt down all the assumptions that have not been tested out. That's why we all need grace to grow.

Parts of the Body of Christ

Several years ago, I was in Aruba on vacation when the Lord showed me why I wanted to quit pastoring to just work my business and travel and preach as an itinerant minister. I had built my leadership on the wrong blueprint. He asked me a simple question: "If your purpose is to bring heaven to earth, why do you focus so much on the fivefold offices?" He said that the fivefold offices are not eternal; they are necessary to equip the saints and bring them into maturity in Christ, but you don't see apostles and prophets in heaven.

He continued to show me that the people who held those positions of apostles and prophets on earth are elders and saints in heaven. This was news to me because I had worked hard building all of the five-fold offices in my church with their differences, functions, and placement in the body. So I went back to my church and restructured the leadership to be governed by husband and wife elder teams. This took several years to work through the dynamic and relational changes. In the process, we lost a lot of title-driven leaders who couldn't make the change.

It was time to flesh out an elder-governed body. At Identity Church, this is the personal blueprint from heaven for us. We govern as equals with different strengths, then we apply the giftings of the five-fold offices that we have within our eldership and the body, and come into agreement when we need outside help through relationships we have built. This was a several-year process to build and make foundationally sound. It has been tested in the fire and proven to be the Lord's plan for us.

One morning in prayer, the Lord started to reveal portions of the Word to me about how we are a body and many members.

> For just as the body is one and has many members, and all the members of the body, though man, are one body, so it is with Christ (1 Corinthians 12:12)
>
> For as in one body we have many members, and the members do not all have the same function, so we, though many, are one body in Christ, and individually members of one another (Romans 12:4–5).

The Lord asked me to look at my physical body and apply these passages. My hands and feet are needed to walk and function in life. I examined how my eyes and ears are needed to give information to my brain, and that one part to the other is totally connected. I have hidden organs that have to function with each other or I would die; I have veins and a nervous system all working for the same goals.

Then He interrupted me and asked, "Hey, what would you look like if you didn't have any bones?"

I said that I would be a big blob of flesh and muscle, mixed with body parts that had no way of working together.

THE BOUNDARIES OF GRACE

The Lord said that the source of some of my frustration with my church is that I didn't honor the bones like He did. I have an all-in personality, and that became religious legalism. Then I found the grace message and abandoned structure to the point where it was sloppy grace without proper boundaries.

He started reviewing with me that it's the finished work of the cross where grace and innocence is released to the body of Christ. The Lord said that if I would honor the bones as much as He did, I could find the balance to bring myself and the church into maturity with the image of Jesus Christ.

He started showing me that without the bones being honored, my ministry will never be generational and will die off when I die or stop ministering. He then said that He honored the bone so much, that He put in the Scriptures that not one of His bones were broken.

> Since it was the day of Preparation, and so that the bodies would not remain on the cross on the Sabbath (for that Sabbath was a high day), the Jews asked Pilate that their legs might be broken and that they might be taken away. So the soldiers came and broke the legs of the first, and of the other who had been crucified with him. But when they came to Jesus and saw that he was already dead, they did not break his legs. But one of the soldiers pierced his side with a spear, and at once there came out blood and water. He who saw it has borne witness—his testimony is true, and he knows that he is telling the truth—that you also may believe. For these things took place that the Scripture might be fulfilled: "Not one of his bones will be broken." And again another Scripture says, "They will look on him whom they have pierced" (John 19:31–37).

The Lord showed me that I had taken love past its boundaries and would sacrifice the bones (structure) of the church and family. Love out of balance will become control and is detrimental to the family. It is just like when we had to deal with addictions in our family that would have ripped our family apart, but we became a place to return and find a family structure where healing and deliverance was experienced. The church needs the same bones not to be broken, or grace and innocence will not be an advantage, but rather destructive and unusable for the kingdom of God.

Jesus said to me that the spirit of wisdom is given to the people of God to know when to die, or when to surrender, change, protect, or release, before the bones are broken, in order to become a generational inheritance and hand it to others to finish the race.

***

Wisdom Keys:

1. When your identity comes into alignment with Christ and the Father, behavior and lifestyle will follow.
2. Grace is an offensive empowerment to holiness, not a defensive excuse to walk in sin.

Chapter 8: Childlikeness Is the Weapon!

As I have worked through the mechanics and the applications of innocence, I have found that it is a major ingredient to bring us into maturity and Christlikeness. I have also found that it is not and cannot stand alone, or it will become an excuse to stay immature and unproductive in the kingdom. But discovering childlikeness is one of the core components. As I was walking this out, my friend Brian Higbee said to me that I was childlike in my walk with God. We were with a group of close friends as we discussed this statement. At the time, I totally disagreed with them about me being childlike.

It became very apparent that I didn't have grid on what childlikeness was, even though I was in some ways.

Blind Obedience

The first thing that they pointed out was that when I hear God say something, I obey Him, almost with a blind faith. Many times, I obey in a moment with no hesitation. I do hear God clearly, but they believed my childlikeness empowered me with the ability to obey and trust God for the outcome. So they said I am childlike with a blind faith that trusts the Father.

But on the other side, they have always been puzzled how I argue with God when I disagree with Him. My closest friends have always felt as though I have a different relationship with Him that gives me a "free pass" to challenge the Father if I disagreed to be able to

THE BAPTISM OF INNOCENCE

argue with Him. In that regard, many of my friends have accused me of being disrespectful toward the Lord. As we openly discussed what childlikeness was, they fit this portion of my relationship with God also into childlikeness by just looking at our own children and how they interact with us as parents.

We don't raise robots; we raise children who can think and act on their own. We give them the skillset to be critical thinkers, and many times as they mature, they challenge us as parents. That forced me to revisit what I say I believe, because my actions were not lining up to my beliefs. Many times, I would find hidden assumptions that were eroding my beliefs and fueling bad behavior.

My friends also noted that when I was done debating with God and He pulled His "God Card," I would obey, even if I disagreed. But my childlike curiosity would make me inspect the issue to find what I was missing and learn from it. When I disagreed with God, whether it is spiritual or natural, there is a tendency in me to seek things out; it taps into the all-knowing side of God. He is not hiding from me, but wants me to pursue Him for the truth that is hidden from others. I call it Holy Spirit "hide and seek."

> It is the glory of God to conceal things, but the glory of kings is to search things out (Prov. 25:2).

As we continued talking about how I am childlike, my friend Brian mentioned Gideon. In Judges 8, Gideon's son Jether was raised to be a prince, and not a king. So when it was time to use the sword, he shrunk back. When you raise your children to only be princes, they will not have the tools to be kings and priests, and they won't be able to fulfill their destiny as such. Insecure leaders only want princes around them to serve their kingdom. The Bible tells us to raise kings and priests. The position of a prince should be temporary—a learning stage with the goal to see ourselves as kings. When we don't release childlikeness, we are not going to have the God-given ability to even imagine seeing ourselves as kings the way the Father sees us. The religious spirit will try and kill the imagination that childlikeness brings into our maturing process.

Accepting of Others

One of the other traits of childlikeness that I carry is the ability to accept others quickly. Brian Higbee used the first time we met as an example of this childlikeness.

I was coming to my first sons gathering with Papa Jack in North Carolina, and when I saw Brian Higbee walk into the room, the Lord highlighted him to me. When we shook hands, there was a supernatural connection. I like to say that he "made my baby jump"! The Lord spoke to me and said, "This man will become a covenant brother, a lifetime relationship." I was all in. Anybody the Father approves is okay with me, warts and all, and when you can make my "baby jump," that means you got something on the inside of you that I need, and vice versa.

But Brian, not having as much childlikeness, did not have the same response as I did. He says that he did not like me at first. He was turned off at my boldness and labeled me like others who had blown in and out of his life. My childlikeness kept me pursuing him with an open heart. A few days later we were sitting around a fire, and Brian's prophetic gift started kicked in. He began telling me who I was in the Spirit and exposing some of my weaknesses. You can be sure that when iron sharpens iron, there will be sparks! If I had not heard God and trusted with childlikeness, it could have been offensive, but I believe God was showing Brian that I had the goods, and that he was to engage with me in relationship. I can tell you he is one of my most-trusted confidants and friend—I trust him with my life and ministry.

Humor

Childlikeness also gives you a sense of humor. When I first ran into Mary and Jim Baker, there was this resistance to the anointing they carried (that I now know was innocence). But what puzzled me was when I was trying to falsely accuse them of being religious, they had such a great sense of humor. They are hilarious people!

THE BAPTISM OF INNOCENCE

It's funny how much Susie and I have used humor to get over horrific stuff in our lives. It helps to have childlike humor so you don't take yourself too seriously.

I remember a trip that we were on, when one of my worship leaders, Kevin, was riding with us. Our silly humor kicked in and Susie and I started picking on each other about our mothers. Both are in heaven, and both of us were the babies of our families. I started telling Susie that my mother's mansion was so big that her mother was my mother's house cleaner in heaven. She rebounded by saying that my mother didn't get her crippled hand healed, and that was why her mother had to clean for her, and that her mother was God's favorite and got healing from her crippled feet, and that she was Christlike and served my mother out of love, but my mother only wanted a slave to clean.

This went on for a while and Kevin started yelling, "Hey, I'm back here. Stop it. You two are crazy!" For years he said that you had to experience our humor firsthand or you would have thought it was sacrilegious and disrespectful. Only childlike imagination with humor would argue over whose mother was better off in heaven. (Our mothers were prayer partners when Susie and I were in our darkest times.)

Generosity

Childlikeness makes one generous. I have been so generous at times that I put my family into financial problems. But God was also taking the love of money out of me, trying to bring me into balance in my giving. When you trust God the Father like a child, there is a lack of concern with how are you going to be taken care of.

I have always been faithful in my giving, but until innocence came into the picture, I didn't see that childlikeness kills off fear and anxiety. I have always used the principles of sowing and reaping to my advantage. It works, and I will continue to live it and teach it, but innocence made me reexamine my beliefs and behaviors when it came to money. True childlikeness that is fueled by innocence causes fear and anxiety to have no place. The Lord showed me a picture of a child in a good home. The child was playing and having a great time enjoying life. As I looked, the child was not worried about the mortgage payment or if the light bill was late and the power was going to get turned off. A child trusts his parents that those things would automatically be handled. That's the way we should feel with Father God. My new childlikeness being renewed with innocence has helped me not to be driven to make money out of fear. Therefore, childlike faith that is fueled by innocence has brought contentment in my life.

True Humility

Childlikeness is the foundation of true humility. I want to share a story about a broken relationship that has taken over twenty-two years for the Lord to heal. This is a good example of how innocence, along with the application of childlikeness, are the major tools that the Lord is using to fix broken relationships within the body of Christ.

Twenty-five years ago, I was sent by the Father into a region with specific boundaries in upstate New York. He gave me the instructions to fly to Buffalo, New York, on a Friday and fly home on Monday nights once a month. Through this He would show me how the kingdom works. He also showed me promises of a great move of His Spirit and revival in those regions. He gave me relationships within the area, and God was personally teaching me how to function as a prophet.

To make a long story short, I had made some very personal relationships within the church, and during one weekend of ministry I gave a word that was strong and corrective in nature. Without going into detail, the pastor and the leadership rejected my word and called me a false prophet. I didn't handle that very well and tried to defend myself, destroying those relationships. On top of that, I was reprimanded by my overseers and taken out of ministry for a season.

After a few years, I asked for forgiveness on seven different occasions. I believe forgiveness was given, but there was no foundation or trust to have any further relationship.

THE BAPTISM OF INNOCENCE

This is where another trait of childlikeness comes into play, where it gives us the ability to get up, even after a great fall. After twenty-two years, this pastor and I wound up in the same meeting, and while we were there, a prophet had a word for us both. He had us stand back to back and started prophesying that a "whispering prophet" brought division to us. He said that this pastor was an apostle who God called to open a door of revival, and that I was a key to some of the promises of revival in that region. He had very specific information revealing to us that we both knew who the whispering prophet was. This man who was prophesying over us said he had asked the Lord who it was, and the Lord told him that the man had passed away. He also knew information about my mother's prayers, and this pastor and I were convinced that God was trying to heal our relationship now, twenty-two years later.

After the meeting, we spoke about what to do next and we made plans to meet. I had a date during a conference that worked for me and Rodney, one of my elders who would be traveling with me, and we made time to sit down with the pastor and some of his elders.

Before the meeting, I was praying and asking God what to expect and how to re-engage with this man after so many years. The Lord had me go through the paperwork that I still had in my heart against him and get rid of it, then release innocence on this pastor personally and his eldership. The Lord had me send it ahead of this meeting like a holy weapon into the hearts of those coming.

The meeting was from heaven! It was like I walked into the room, and all the paperwork was gone on both sides. I repented for my behavior as an immature prophet and asked for forgiveness one more time. This time humility showed up like I'd never had before, and the leadership saw it and responded in like manner. As we were ending the meeting in prayer, one of the elders got on floor and prayed that God would bless every place where my feet touched the ground.

As Rodney and I got into the truck to leave, I asked, "What in the world just happened?"

CHILDLIKENESS IS THE WEAPON!

He said prophetically, "When your humility is bigger than your boldness, then God can use you to expand the kingdom and heal relationships."

We did our conference and, through some unusual circumstances, ended up at that pastor's church on Sunday morning. God had a plan to finish the healing process. By the end of the day, a twenty-two-year relationship was being healed. He even asked when I could come preach this message of innocence to his church.

Take a look at what his social media post from that night said:

> Crazy, unpredictable, awesome, no one thought would, should, or could happen kind of day! The devil limped away from church today! And most of those present had NO IDEA how much of a God-ordained collision it was. The power of forgiveness!

You might be saying, "Great story, Charlie, but what does childlikeness have to do with humility?" Let's look at Moses, who put it in the Bible.

> Then Miriam and Aaron spoke against Moses because of the Ethiopian woman whom he had married; for he had married an Ethiopian woman. So they said, "Has the Lord indeed spoken only through Moses? Has He not spoken through us also?" And the Lord heard it. **(Now the man Moses was very humble, more than all men who were on the face of the earth.)** Suddenly the Lord said to Moses, Aaron, and Miriam, "Come out, you three, to the tabernacle of meeting!" So, the three came out. Then the Lord came down in the pillar of cloud and stood in the door of the tabernacle and called Aaron and Miriam. And they both went forward. Then He said, "Hear now My words: If there is a prophet among you, I, the Lord, make Myself known to him in a vision; I speak to him in a dream. Not so with My servant Moses; He is faithful in all My house. I speak with him

face to face, even plainly, and not in dark sayings; and he sees the form of the Lord. Why then were you not afraid to speak against My servant Moses?" So the anger of the Lord was aroused against them, and He departed (Num. 12:1–9 NKJV, emphasis mine).

The book of Numbers was written by Moses. If I wrote a book and said about myself that I was the most humble man in the face of the earth, many people would loudly accuse me of arrogance and pride, saying that I proclaimed it just to look good because humility is a known character requirement of the Lord. But innocence and childlikeness are the foundations for those who have dealt with the fear and insecurity that comes with a great calling. When you have the wrong fuel for motivation, it is seen as pride and arrogance—even when you ask for forgiveness.

Innocence goes beyond forgiveness and brings childlikeness and gratitude that the Father would trust you with a great calling to display His love to the world. And that, my friend, is humbling! It also causes others to see it in a new light.

Just to summarize, I have listed the attributes of childlikeness in a handy list below:

1. Blind obedience—trusting the Father.
2. Can debate with the Father with honor and respect.
3. Curiosity: to find wisdom and truth.
4. Having an imagination to see what the Father sees.
5. Accepting others quickly; we learn to trust others by the Spirit.
6. Having a sense of humor.
7. Giving generously.
8. Being content.
9. Getting up after a fall.
10. Foundation for true humility.

***

Wisdom Keys:

1. Innocence can be sent ahead of you as a weapon in your time of intercession.
2. When your humility is bigger than your boldness, then God can use you.

Chapter 9: It's About the Lamb, Not a Goat

As I was working out this new revelation with the baptism of innocence, I would call and talk to my father on the matter. My dad was a very committed Christian and had complete chapters of the Bible memorized. If you read my first book, *Church Fathers vs. Kingdom Sons: The Inheritance Worth Fighting For*, you will find in detail the kind of relationship we had. My father was a good man with spiritual convictions which made him a leader in the church world and good father. But when it came to his children not living up to his expectations and beliefs of what the Lord required, there was always a fight with the religious spirit that we, as his children, had to learn to manage to keep peace within the family.

Mom's Prophetic Insight

Three weeks before my mother passed on and went home to be with the Lord, she called me and asked to see me privately before her heart operation the next day. As I hung up the phone, I went into a vision and saw seats of authority in my family changing positions. I saw that my mother's seat was being removed, then I saw that my father was seated in the patriarchal seat of authority above the whole family. I saw that my sisters' seat of authority stayed in place, my father's seat was being lowered, and my seat of authority was lifted above my father's. As I hung up the phone, I knew that my mother was not going to make it through the operation and that the spiritual family structure was about to change.

THE BAPTISM OF INNOCENCE

I drove across the state of Florida to the West Coast where they were going to do exploratory surgery. My mother had several issues from a previous bypass surgery not working, and she has been given up for dead more than once. For over fifteen years she had confounded the medical community because of how well she has done, and my father was an amazing caregiver for her.

As I drove, I recalled that she'd had her first heart attack in the 80s while driving down the road. A police officer found her slumped over the steering wheel where she had a heart attack and died and went to heaven. During that experience, Jesus asked her if she was ready to come home and be with Him, and she made a deal with God that if she could see all of her children serving the Lord before she died, that would be the only reason for her to stay on earth.

I am the youngest of four children and the only male, and I was born on my mother's birthday. To say the least, I was a momma's boy and her favorite. At the time, I was not serving God; I was in the middle of becoming a total reprobate and was heading through all the stages of blaspheming the Holy Spirit. Hearing the deal my mother made with God about all her children serving Christ only made me run harder away from Him.

The doctor in the emergency room asked my father if he could try a new experimental drug that they shoot right into the heart. It worked and she recovered. She had many surgeries and did well for years.

I remember when one of her bypass surgeries had failed. We were in the Orlando Hospital when the doctor came into the room with a chart showing that all three of the bypasses had collapsed, and said that they could keep her comfortable for a few weeks at that most. He instructed us to call the family and prepare for her to pass, and that they couldn't do anything else for her. I looked at the doctor and then pointed to my mother and aggressively made this statement. "She will not die. We all know the deal she made with God, and we all know that I'm not serving God."

I walked out of the room and my mother started yelling for me to come back. She pointed a finger in my face and said, "Maybe I will make a deal with God and have Him zap you so He can take you to heaven right now."

I asked her why God didn't just heal her and stop all the pain. She looked at me and said, "Baby, I have prayed for three nurses to receive Christ in the last ten days. If that is the only good that comes from this, then I am blessed."

As I reminisced, I felt that this was becoming one of the longest drives of my life. I pleaded with the Lord and asked if this was negotiable. He said, "No, it's her time." I wondered why my mother wanted to see me privately the day before her operation.

When I arrived, my mother had everyone leave the room, and she started talking to me about how the other night she had gone to heaven and walked with Jesus. They stopped and looked over a balcony and Jesus showed her my life and ministry. Then she gave me stern instructions and said that if I disobeyed them, my ministry would never be successful.

The instructions were about my father. She said that my father was a man of faith, but not a man of the Spirit, and that he was going to try and destroy the gifting that I carry. Then she looked at me with eyes that pierced my soul and said, "Charles, if you don't learn to do war with honor, you will never win your father's favor. But when you do, the day will come when he will truly see who you are and who you are called by God to be, and then he will serve you." She continued, saying, "This is your test to pass or fail, not his."

She had the surgery and had a stroke, passing on three weeks later. That was in March of 1997.

Fathering Father

So there I was, twenty-two years later. I obeyed my mother's instructions, and at the age of eighty-five, my father called me and started telling me that I had offended him the previous weekend when I made the statement that he was a spiritual orphan. I expected another round of boxing, but he asked me a different question: "When are you going to man up and pray a father's blessing over me, become my spiritual father, and teach me how to know God the Father like you do?" So I started fathering my own father when he was eighty-five years old.

Eight years later, my father had a bicycle accident and then hip replacement, and we had to move him into assisted living. All in all, he did well, being as strong-willed as he was, and having to deal with all the changes. When it came to the hard topics, he consulted with me for moral and spiritual support. I was the elected one of the family to reason with Dad when we had to make the hard choices.

So at ninety-two, my father sold the house that he had raised us in and lived in for over fifty years to move into an assisted living facility. Selling his home was very traumatic for him; it made it permanent that he would never be living on his own again. My father has always been a leader in the church and a very committed Christian. He loved the Lord very much, but could be over-religious and legalistic, to say the least.

"Goat" Issues

I had been sharing with him for several weeks about the revelation of the baptism of innocence and all the verses proving what Christ gave us through His death on the cross. As we have been talking about, it is foundational that all Christian truths have to start with innocence, to stay pure and righteous.

My father had a family issue that had changed his attitude and feelings for one of his granddaughters. He had loaned her $7,000.00 so she and her husband could purchase a new sire goat to get a better bloodline in their herd. The crazy thing was that they didn't ask for the money; Dad offered it. Like always, Dad went to his accountant and had loan documents drawn up with the payment dates. He added a very small amount of interest to be paid over a three-year period.

However, a few months into the process, the goat died. (Dad joked that the goat died happily doing his job.) They made payments for a while, but fell on hard times. Eventually the payments slowed and weren't consistent, and then stopped altogether with different promises. On several talks with Dad, I told him to write it off. I would tell my father, "You're a millionaire; write it off!" I would say, "Dad, it's starting to harden your heart and is making you bitter toward your granddaughter."

After a long while, she said that she had sent a check for $1000.00, but it came back in the mail, even though she had used the correct address. My father was a retired postmaster, so that didn't hold water. Then after a while, she came to visit and asked if she could make payments of fifty dollar per month, to which they agreed on but never completed.

Family Crisis

This had developed over years and was starting to turn my father's heart against not only my niece, but it even started affecting his relationship with my older sister, who is an accountant and takes care of his money and pays all his bills. The fact is that this bitterness and unforgiveness against my niece was clouding his vision toward everyone involved. The whole family felt it; we spoke about it and prayed, asking God how to handle this issue that was starting to destroy a Christian family at its core.

My father's accusations were clearly driven from bitterness, and were not in line with our family values. This got my sister Margret upset to the point that she was going to stop handling his finances. Now the rest of us truly started praying! Margret was his favorite, and if she fell from grace, there was little hope for the rest of us. He even asked my wife, Susie, if she would handle his finances, to which she adamantly refused.

Many people would say because he was ninety-two years old that he was starting to lose his mental capacity with dementia or some other aging issue. But that was not the case with my father—his mind was as sharp as a tack. During the last few months before he passed away, I witnessed just how sharp his mind was when my sister started telling him all the checks she had written for him over the last few months. She rattled off about twenty-five checks, who they went to and the amounts. While she spoke, he was calculating all the totals in his head. When she finished, he asked if his retirement check was deposited in that account or another. Then he asked what the amount of a dividend check from some stocks had come in and how much that was. After she responded, He looked up in the air and said, "There should be $22,357.55 in that account." He was only three dollars off from what was actually in that account. It was amazing! So don't think we were some ungrateful kids making this stuff up. Bitterness was destroying this family.

The situation between my father and my sister was turning into a disaster, and it was becoming apparent that if something didn't change, she was about to walk away from the responsibility. My father's bitterness and unforgiveness had gone past the point of no return and was bringing us into irreparable damage. This once-strong Christian family was in a crisis.

I watched the emotions within a family group text, and it became apparent that only the Lord could heal this gash in our family. It was bringing to the surface over sixty years of spiritual abuse. As I prayed for a strategy to get this resolved, the Lord showed me that the baptism of innocence was the key. I prayed and told God that throughout my whole life my father and I had never been able to confront an issue in a civil manner. The Lord told me that He was going before me and was preparing my father's heart.

Getting Rid of the Paperwork

I had to drive two hours to take my dad to the attorney's office, the bank, and then we went to lunch together. We were sitting in the parking lot of a BBQ restaurant to have lunch when I said, "Dad, I need to talk to you about something very important. I'm not talking to you as your son, but as a pastor." He said okay.

IT'S ABOUT THE LAMB, NOT A GOAT

I asked my father if he had worked through the revelation I had been sharing with him for weeks about the baptism of innocence. He said that he had, and that it was what Jesus completed for all of us on the cross.

Then I asked if he had received the baptism of innocence for himself. His reply was, "Yes, I am innocent because of the finished work of the cross."

I asked if he could prove it and he looked at me with a puzzled look.

"How do I prove it?" he replied.

I said, "If you have received it from the Lord, the only way to prove it is to give it away." Then I asked if he could declare his granddaughter innocent from the debt that was never repaid. At that point he started to manifest bitterness and unforgiveness, and he broke down and cried. (I had to do some deliverance right there in the car.) I had never seen him cry with true repentance in my life. This was completely new territory for me and my father.

With his brokenness, I gave him the plan that the Lord had shown me.

I asked Dad if we could go back to his assisted-living apartment after lunch and let me serve him communion and ask for forgiveness for the bitterness and resentment in his heart. This would also include writing a letter to forgive his granddaughter and her husband of the debt that was owed. He then started telling me a story that before Susie and I went to prepare his house to be sold, he had asked my cousin to take him by the house. He had taken the folder containing all the paperwork from his accountant with all the checks and loan payments, deposits, and handwritten notes of promises made and not been followed through with. He had truly kept all the record of wrong that had been done to him—all the paperwork.

When we got to his assisted-living apartment, he pulled out the paperwork and showed me all the details that the enemy had been tormenting his mind with. He told me that a demon was in those papers and that he had realized a few weeks earlier that his heart was not right, and right then he asked God for help to dealing with his bitterness and unforgiveness—weeks before I was confronting him with letting it go.

After communion and prayer of repentance, he took the paperwork and asked me what to write. "Forgiveness of debt," or "Paid in full," I instructed. Then I added, "Dad, forgiveness of debt still has a record, but innocence declares that it is 'paid in full.'" We also wrote a short letter which told his granddaughter what he had done, asked for forgiveness, said that he was sorry, and pronounced a blessing over her and her husband.

Then he asked me to take all that paperwork and get it out of his apartment. As we were finishing and I was about to leave, he asked me to sit down as he pulled his wheelchair up close to me.

He said, "Charlie, you have always been a good son. God has made you a strong prophet, but today you were a great pastor because you wouldn't allow me to live this Christian life with my heart full of bitterness." He thanked me for caring enough to help him get it right with God and his family. This changed his total demeanor and there was light and life back in his soul!

Innocence at a Funeral

As I traveled for ministry and business the next week, I preached this message on the baptism of innocence and told the story about my father and the goat issue, and how the baptism of innocence was the key to healing our family. I had my pastor friend drive me from Pittsburg to Philadelphia for a few days of business, and was at the airport heading home when I called my father.

Whenever I would call my dad, I would ask, "How are you doing?" For the last few years he always replied with humor and would say, "At my age, every day above dirt is a good day," or, "Getting old isn't for sissies." Today when I called and asked how he was doing he replied, "I'm innocent, how about you?" I told him that I had shared his story of getting free and how God really touched people's hearts, that many people came to the altar, and a lot of healing took place. Then said,

IT'S ABOUT THE LAMB, NOT A GOAT

"Dad, I would like to preach this at your funeral." He asked why and I said that at his age, most people can't hear God's voice or are willing to repent. I told him, "I have never been prouder of you. It made my heart jump to see how you allowed God to heal you and our family."

So dad gave me permission to preach the baptism of innocence at his funeral, but he added that it wouldn't be anytime soon! It was Wednesday afternoon. As I hung up, I had this thought: *He got it!*

Early Friday morning I got a phone call that my dad had a stroke. He passed away a few days later. We had his funeral on his ninety-third birthday. I preached the message on the baptism of innocence and told the goat story. The church was packed, and to say the least, there were some people who were unhappy with me because they had put my father on a Christian pedestal; they felt that I had exposed his sin and dishonored him. There were people who had only seen him in the church world, but had never lived under his rule. He was hard to live with because he had a religious spirit that would murder you if you crossed him. So my opinion of the greatest accomplishment my father had toward his family became a criticism of me and an accusation that I dishonored him.

This disapproval did not help my grieving process.

Three weeks after his funeral, I was on a trip to Texas and had a prophetic encounter in heaven with my father. As I went into heaven, Jesus met me. I asked Jesus what He wanted, and He told me that my father wanted some private time with me. I was led into a room with no windows, just a door on the opposite side of the room. As I waited, my mind started wondering with all the thoughts of my childhood, and I was very curious what my father wanted to see me about—and privately to boot!

The door opened and my father walked into the room. He was about thirty-five years old and a man's man—broad shoulders, very strong looking, and fit. He had a huge, brilliant green bowl of fruit in his arms. He looked at me and said that he was proud of me and told me that he loved me. I looked into this green bowl that was filled with the most succulent fruit I had ever seen. He offered me some of his fruit. As I tasted this fruit, it was full of energy and life and it felt like light shot out of this fruit and energized my whole body. I said that was the best fruit I had ever tasted (in the natural, I don't eat fruit a lot) and he offered me another handful.

As I finished the fruit, I asked what he wanted to see me about. He said that he had a problem in heaven, and needed my help. I looked with puzzlement and disgust and said, "Dad, you're the only person I know who would finally get to heaven and have a problem! What is your problem?"

He said it was the fruit. He said, "Son, you're supposed to show up in heaven with crowns with jewels in them." Then he said, "Don't get me wrong, I have some of those, but this fruit is the problem. Son, this fruit is what I should have shared with you all those years when I kept you at arm's length. When you had your encounters with God the way you did, it scared me—and the fear of man kept me from engaging with you when you needed me the most. I kept that part of my relationship with God to myself, and did not share how to walk in the fruit of the Spirit with you or others." Then he asked if I could help him with his fruit issue and he told me to write a book.

As I came out of that encounter, I asked Jesus what it was all about. The Lord said that the title of the book will be called, *Your Hero, My Father: the Journey of a Righteous Man.* As I sat and pondered what that would look like, the Lord started reminding me that my father had turned down the gift of being a prophet to the body of Christ on two occasions, and when he asked me to pray that orphan spirit off of him and asked for me to father him so that he could know the Father like I do, that was the beginning stages of becoming childlike and innocent.

My father lived by his favorite Bible chapter, which was Psalm 37. The whole chapter is a road map to what a righteous man does with his walk with God. And it ends with verse 37 (KJV):

IT'S ABOUT THE LAMB, NOT A GOAT

Mark the perfect man, and behold the upright: for the end of that man is peace.

The word *perfect* is also translated, "blameless, flawless, innocent."

Rest in peace, Papa.

***

Wisdom Keys:

1. Bitterness will destroy even a strong Christian family.
2. You are to show up in heaven with crowns that have jewels in them.
3. You are not to show up in heaven with fruit; you need to give the fruit away on earth to others.

Chapter 10: Operational Instructions for the Weapon of Innocence

I want to note that not all relationships should be repaired. When there is abuse and ungodly behaviors, you deal with your own paperwork, get healing, and be free to grow in Christlikeness personally. God has not ordained every relationship for reconnection. So be led by the Spirit. The baptism of innocence first happens between you and the Holy Spirit for us to stop stiff-arming the Father and allow Him to love us first. Relationship reconciliation is a byproduct of that baptism.

Closing out this book has been the hardest for me, because the longer I walk this out in my Christian life, the more testimonies I have of how good God is, and how He has given us the tools to walk in the ministry of reconciliation in the body of Christ. I believe that this is a major key to bring fulfilment of John 13:31–35:

> A new commandment I give to you, that you love one another; as I have loved you, that you also love one another. By this all will know that you are My disciples, if you have love for one another (John 13:34–35).

This baptism of innocence is key for going past forgiveness into true reconciliation with the Father and then healing broken relationships. Most of us will ask for forgiveness because that's a major issue with the Lord, but some never re-engage to show the world that part of the

THE BAPTISM OF INNOCENCE

finished work of the cross is all about love. That display is what will show the world who God is and how much He loves them.

If you are still walking in the flesh, it's proof that you're not embracing the baptism of innocence. Also, cheap innocence will become a license to a newer version of sloppy grace.

Innocence is a Weapon

If this is a weapon that destroys the enemy's plans, then you must understand and know how to wield the weapon.

The last, and possibly the most important, truth that I want to leave with you about innocence is that when you embrace the baptism of innocence, you are sending it ahead of you into your future. When you let it go ahead, the Lord will pick it up on your behalf and can fight the enemy on your behalf.

I want you to take a moment and reflect with the Holy Spirit to see if there is still something in your heart that makes you stiff-arm God the Father when He tries to love you. If you find that you do, put all the reasons on the table, lean forward, and hear Jesus whisper in your ear, "Receive the baptism of innocence."

Walk in this truth for three days before you try to give it to someone else. This is about you first.

P.S.— Enjoy your new childlikeness!

Oh, and if you hear a voice from heaven saying my whole proper name: "Charles Layton Coker Jr.," please pray for me!

In His service,

Charlie Coker

***

OPERATIONAL INSTRUCTIONS FOR THE WEAPON OF INNOCENCE

Wisdom Keys:

1. It was given to you at the finished work of the cross.
2. The innocent blood gave forgiveness of sin.
3. Jesus's nakedness removed your shame and public humiliation.
4. Jesus decreed innocence at the cross.
5. Childlikeness was birthed through innocence.
6. Childlikeness sits on the seat of righteousness.
7. Innocence will manifest purity and holiness.
8. The Father's protection is released to childlikeness.
9. We win all battles when we are in Christ.
10. Innocence is the foundation of being my brother's keeper.

Other Products by Charlie Coker

Church Fathers vs. Kingdom Sons: Inheritance Worth Fighting For

On the heels of being treated like an orphan by men of God whom he trusted—even his own father—Charlie Coker went into a vision that would change his life forever. In the vision he saw a gym full of boxers in training, sparring together and using various equipment to get ready to fight. On one wall was a poster of an upcoming bout that read "Church Fathers vs. Kingdom Sons."

This vision became the catalyst for Charlie's journey out of orphanhood to learning about the fatherhood of God and his own role in bringing healing and deliverance to the fatherless. Follow Charlie as he discovers an inheritance worth fighting for.

Find out more at www.charliecoker.com.

Other Products by Charlie Coker

From Rape to Righteousness: Redeeming the Bride of Christ

How can someone get past a raw injustice that has been dealt to them—such as rape—and be able to forgive? This is the compelling message found in From Rape to Righteousness. Charlie and Susie Coker reveal their painful past in this very transparent story, and challenge every Christian to clean their own house, and then do the same in the church body as a whole.

Forgiveness is the hinge point of our relationship with Jesus, so we need to be actively pursuing forgiveness in every relationship in our lives—past and present. Only by doing this can we truly find freedom and walk in the righteousness of God—only then will the church truly reflect Jesus to an angry and hurting world.

Find out more at www.charliecoker.com.

Invite Charlie Coker to Speak

Why Should You Invite Charlie to Speak In Your Church?

I have known Charlie Coker for over twenty years now and watched him grow in wisdom and in favor in his prophetic anointing in the most difficult testings of life's situations and circumstances. He is always overcoming and rising above as a champion for God and others, leading the way for many to discover their own identity, purpose, destiny, gifts, and talents. Charlie affords others a safe place of truth through relationship, wrapped beautifully in his uncanny way of loving people unconditionally while dealing with hard realities in order to see them mature and growing into all the things of Christ.

I love this man and his genuine, raw, authentic passion and delivery—both in word and deed. He is one of the rare ones you find in life who always show up, invest, and spur on and believe in you, even when you can't see it yourself.

— **Scott Lowmaster**
Senior Leader Journey Church, President and Founder of the Journey Center, Journey Academy, and the iMatter Foundation and Festival

Charlie can be contacted at Charlie@charliecoker.com or by visiting www.charliecoker.com

About the Author

Charlie and Susie Coker are founders of Identity Church in Deltona, Florida. They have also been in the lighting business for over forty years, concurrently pastoring and traveling in an itinerate ministry role, releasing the light of the Father's glory. They have been married for forty years and have two sons, Jason and Bryan, and five grandchildren.

Charlie and Susie have a unique ability to share the love of God and His healing power because they have walked through the restoration of a broken marriage and broken lives. They started as orphans, dependent on self-works for God's approval, and transitioned into sons of the Father. The guidance of Jack Taylor, their spiritual father, has been vital for this process. They are transparent about their struggles, and bring healing in many areas. Because of the training of the last twenty-five years, they are able to teach others how to rule and reign from a heavenly position.

Charlie's perspective and pursuit of the kingdom of God started in 1993 when King Jesus came to personally visit him. Jesus walked through a wall, asked Charlie to put his hand in His hand, and assured him that He would never leave or forsake him; telling Charlie that otherwise He was going to let hell have its way with him. This introduction to the King and His kingdom gives Charlie a unique insight into how the kingdom of God functions.

Charlie can be contacted at Charlie@charliecoker.com or by visiting www.charliecoker.com

www.ingramcontent.com/pod-product-compliance
Lightning Source LLC
Chambersburg PA
CBHW052054070526